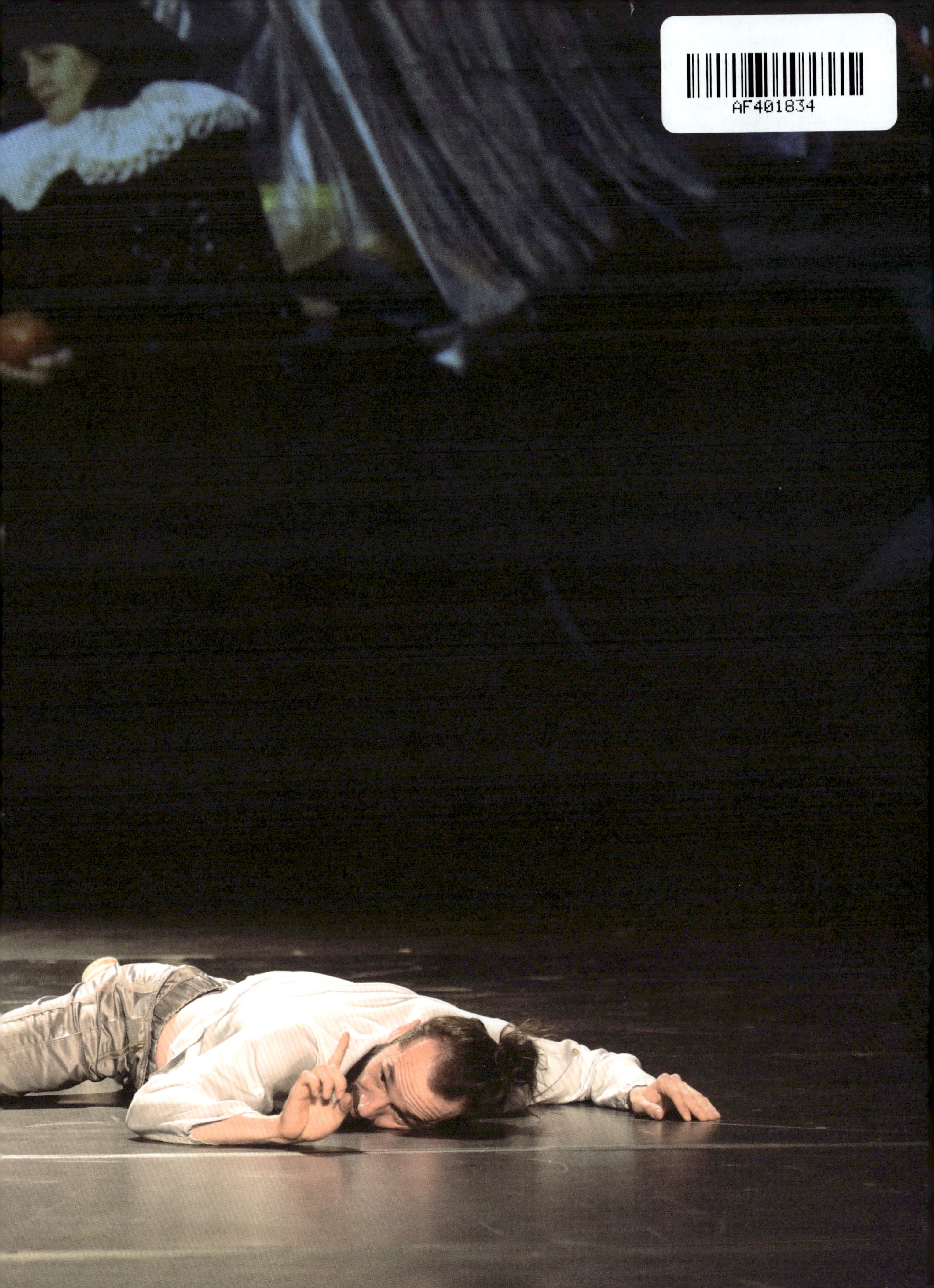
AF401834

DER PALAST

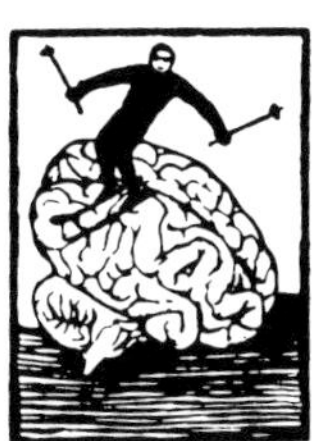

Alexander Verlag Berlin

Alexander Verlag Berlin

DER PALAST

CONSTANZA MACRAS
TOM HUNTER

and
THOMAS AURIN

INDEX

PROLOGUE

by Constanza Macras

I moved to Berlin in the middle of the nineties, semi-casually following a former boyfriend who wanted to make an art project about ghost monuments of the GDR (German Democratic Republic). I was living in Amsterdam at the time, arriving from Buenos Aires. He lived in Frankfurt, arriving from New York. We missed the 24 hour days, the schemes of the megalopolis, the noise, the dirt and everything unexpected and unplanned. Within 10 days in Berlin, we cruised the city inside a Trabant with a municipal list of monuments and their street addresses. Many of the street names had already been changed. What we found when we arrived at most of them was empty ground. The monuments had already been removed as will follow big part of its history.

What we did find was dirt, authentic underground culture, bullet holes in our bedroom walls from the Second World War. We found flexible (even unpredictable) opening hours for restaurants and shops that made us both feel at home. At the same time though, the city's future was an enigma. Potsdamer Platz was the biggest construction site in Europe, and even if we knew that one day there would be buildings to replace the forest of cranes, we preferred to live in denial. We pretended the city would always be under the same construction, always the same.

Berlin Mitte, after the fall of the Wall, was a colorless landscape of dilapidated buildings that was quickly populated as the city absorbed creatives and ravers. Fast forwarding a few decades, this was absorbed into a broader cultural „flattening", made smooth by the taste of an affluent global middle class. Meanwhile, neighborhoods evolved, shops closed and people were evicted from their longstanding homes. Berlin suffered the fate of most every other global metropolis. The city where artists had chosen to live (attracted by cheap rents and deep culture) became a pricey theme park around the narrative of its own history.

"The result of all of this is that the social time available for withdrawing from work and immersing oneself in cultural production drastically declined. If there's one factor above all else which contributes to cultural conservatism, it is the vast inflation in the cost of rent and mortgages. It's no accident that the efflorescence of cultural invention in London and New York in the late 1970s and early 80s (in the punk and postpunk scenes) coincided with the availability of squatted and cheap property in those cities." *(Fisher, Mark. Ghosts of My Life)*

Parallel to the early years of the global gentrification crisis, the raise of syndicated global television formats began to fill the space of entertainment television. Reality TV formats dominated the place of fiction, TV contests like „The voice" became mass culture merchandising in which supposedly real characters could be formatted and copied over and over around the globe, urban planning followed suit. The buildings that emerged in New York, Belgrade and Shanghai were broadly interchangeable.

I created the theater show *Der Palast* in and for this context; the global gentrification not only of cities, but of entertainment and culture itself. Hitting close to the bone, even dance styles themselves became commodified through global TV formats dance reality shows.

Der Palast investigates the impact of this gentrification and its social upheaval, by focusing on the contested architecture, which has stories about the history of the city and its citizens, as well as ideas about the future.
Der Palast translates to 'The Palace' in English; in this context, it refers to the socialist ideal of the People's Palace. The piece was developed for the Volksbühne, a theater that has been at the heart of Berlin during the GDR, and that still now holds some of the last remnants of that time and spirit. Decades prior, my first work at the Volksbühne was actually outside of it: in 2001, the *Rolling Road Show,* created by Bert Neumann and Hannah Hurtzig. It was a caravan that brought the theater to wildly different corners of the city, including Marzahn and Neukölln. Those neighborhoods, at that time, wouldn´t recognize or socialize with the same neighboorhoods today.

I got in contact with Tom Hunter's work through his book "The Way Home". He made a series of photographic works modeled on old masters paintings to draw relationships between the gentrification and squat evictions in Hackney London. We were inspired to invite him to create a new series of photos for *Der Palast.*
Hunter set up photographic tableaus in 10 different urban settings around Berlin, using old master paintings from the Gemäldegalerie as templates to construct new visions of a rapidly changing contemporary city. In these photographic tableaus, Hunter worked with local residents from different housing projects who were facing eviction due to urban redevelopment. Each photograph set the scene and mood for the theatre piece as it developed its narrative and themes of urban flight and regeneration. By referencing old master classics from Berlin´s Gemäldegalerie, and reframing them through a contemporary context of social housing and gentrification, it offered Berlin audiences a way to reflect not only on the past, but the present situation and their future possibilities. The imagination and the management of the urban environment should be somewhere in the hearts and minds of everyone who lives in one.

From this collaboration emerged many things, including this book. Somewhere between an art book and a theater book, it is ultimately our research on a Berlin that always changes, always damned, and always full of possibility.

Ira von Schöppenthau, Jörn Scheele,
Ilja Sutkoff, Almut Zilcher
Der Winter – Lucas van Valckenborch
Tom Hunter, 2019

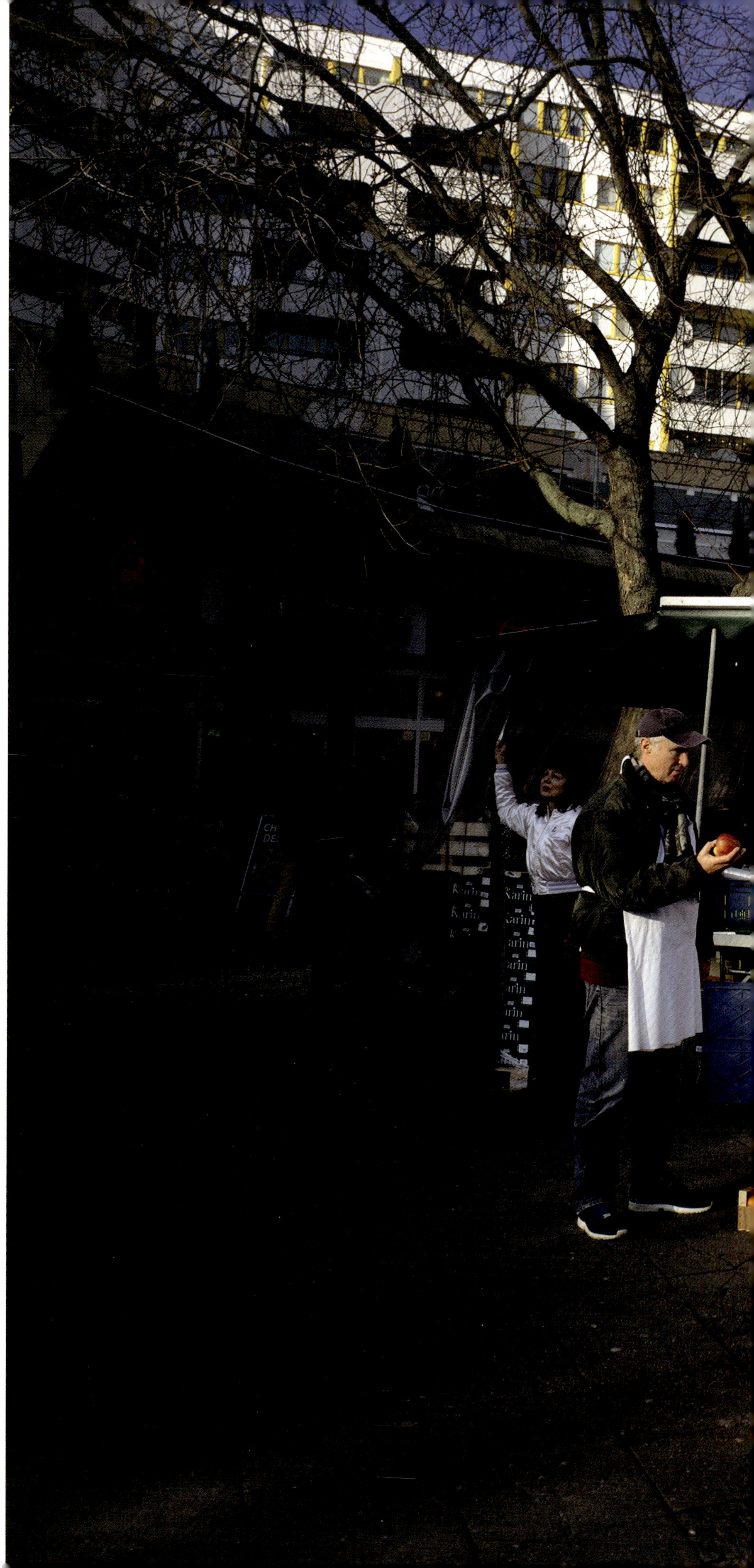

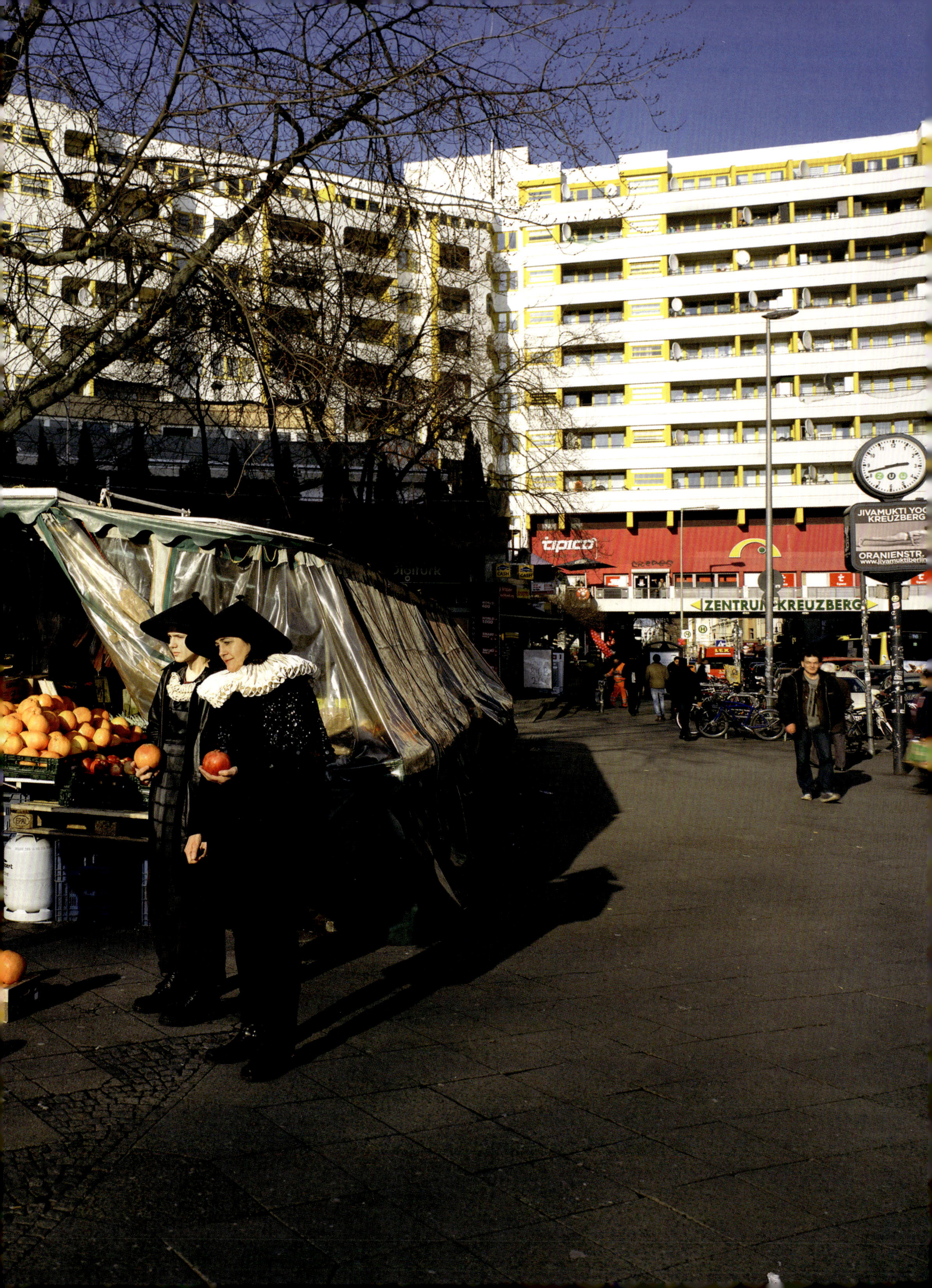

tipico
ZENTRUM KREUZBERG
JIVAMUKTI YOG
KREUZBERG
ORANIENSTR
www.jivamuktiberlin

BERLIN VIGNETTES

by Tom Hunter

Berlin has always been a place resonating with energy and vibrancy for me. My first experience of the city was in 1996 when I arrived there in my double decker bus 'Le Crowbar'. I was travelling around Europe at the time with other people from the UK who had fled there after the suppression of free festivals in the UK. We went from place to place putting on parties, events and festivals. It was at one of these events that we were invited to Berlin to run a bar from the bus for a show taking place in the Arena. It was a mind-blowing experience, visiting Berlin in full transformation from a divided city to a cultural explosion of arts and creativity. The underground scene was brimming with life on a scale I have never seen anywhere else in the world.

Fast forward to 2015 and I'm invited back to Berlin by Constanza Macras and DorkyPark to work on a dance-theatre performance investigating the changing face of Berlin and its rapid gentrification since the heady days of the 1990's and the fall of the Berlin wall. Following mass destruction of Berlin during the second World War the city was divided. East Berlin became part of the communist German Democratic Republic (GDR) whilst West Berlin became part of capitalist West Germany; an isolated island amongst the sea of the GDR. Under the GDR, East Berlin became a showcase for the socialist aspirations and communist utopia, this vision manifested itself in the housing projects that were built for the workers of the GDR. The architecture of these developments stands out as a monument to the utopian dream of socialism though they are now the battlegrounds of commercial developers who are cherry picking the best of them to make huge profits and change the social order of Berlin citizens. The dance piece *Der Palast* sets out to challenge this by giving their communities a voice before they are lost forever. Over the course of three years different resident groups were contacted and stories of the impact of gentrification were collected and written into the narrative of *Der Palast*.

My photographs are architectural studies of 'the palaces' that house the people of Berlin. By staging tableaux images in real life locations, such as the extreme modernist architecture of Marzahn district in East Berlin and the neo-classical architecture of Karl Marx Allee, or the postmodern formations of Kottbusser Tor, I used different styles of architecture and periods of the Soviet post-war utopian dream as a backdrop to highlight the social struggles of its people within these settings. The residents from these developments were arranged to reflect the art historical paintings in the Gemäldegalerie. By combining the architecture, the actual residents of the palaces and the art historical paintings I wanted to encourage the people of Berlin to engage with their city's historical culture in terms of the past, present and future. In this respect it was of vital importance to use the real people from the housing projects, the real locations of their homes and project them back to the people of Berlin. My portraits present social topics in the style of the old masters. They were developed into a series of large-scale photographs that were projected as 40 by 50 foot backgrounds, setting the scene for the performance of *Der Palast*. The staging of *Der Palast* in the Volksbühne (meaning the People's theatre) is also of importance as it is situated within the centre of the old East Berlin and is the main theatre for the East of the city.

Boundaries between the theatre stage and the audience have previously been explored by Bertolt Brecht (1898 – 1956). Using visual devices such as stripping the stage of backdrops whilst breaking the illusion of familiar reality, Brecht makes the viewer question the role of theatre and its relationship to the here and now of social and material subsistence. *Der Palast* follows in Brecht's path but rather than baring the stage - my large scale projected images are used to set the scenes and achieve the effect of completely immersing the audience, transporting them to real life locations within their city – and only then - abruptly breaking that illusion by pulling the viewer back into the theatre distancing them from the experience. A Brechtian toolkit is thus put to work in the very core of this piece.

Whereas my previous work involved incorporating classical paintings inside contemporary photo-montage, this project takes them out and beyond the art gallery context altogether and delivers latent Berlin vignettes to modern theatre audiences that will have an opportunity to perceive them within an immersive multimedia milieu.

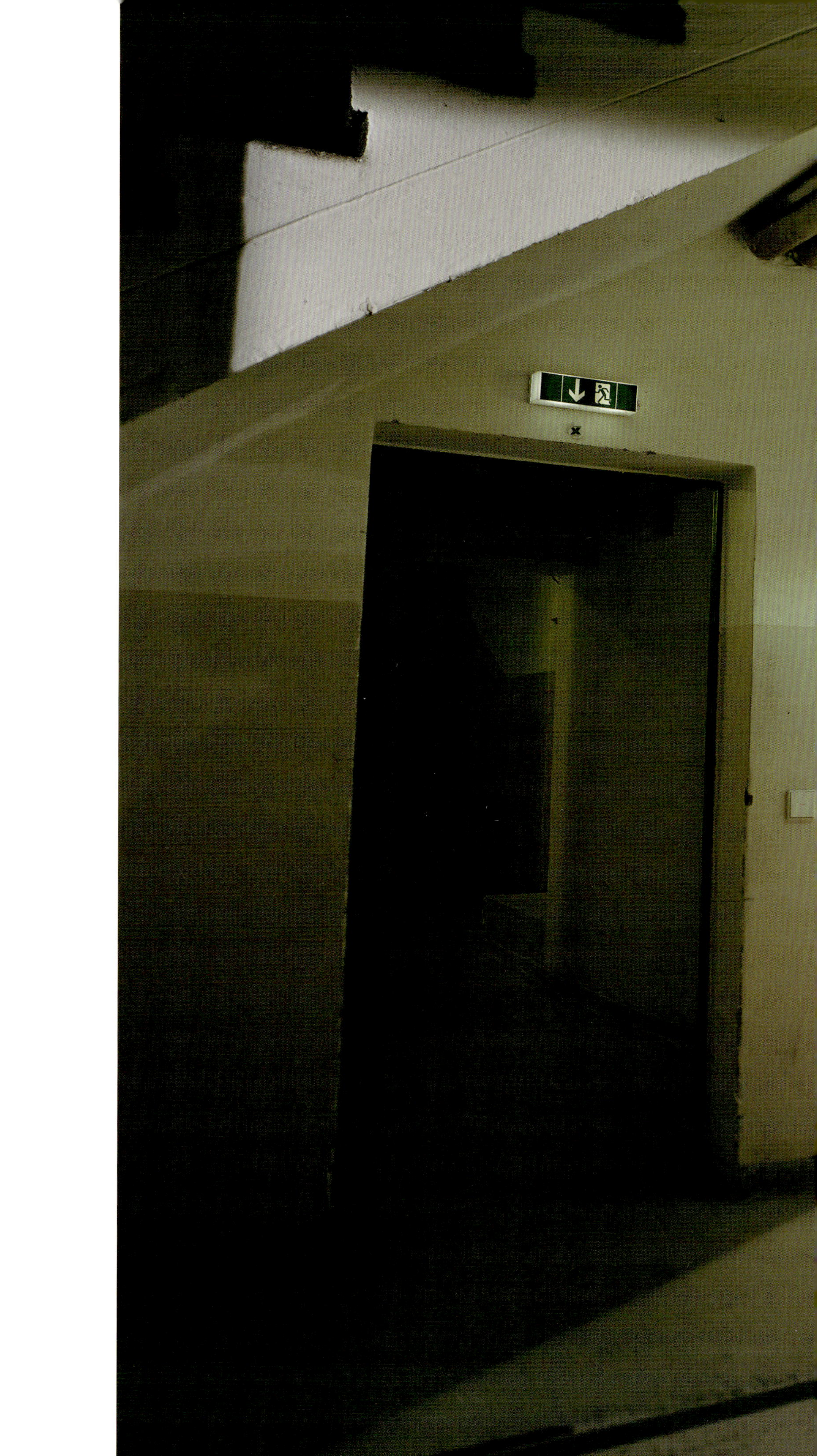

Fernanda Farah
Venus – Boticcelli
Tom Hunter, 2019

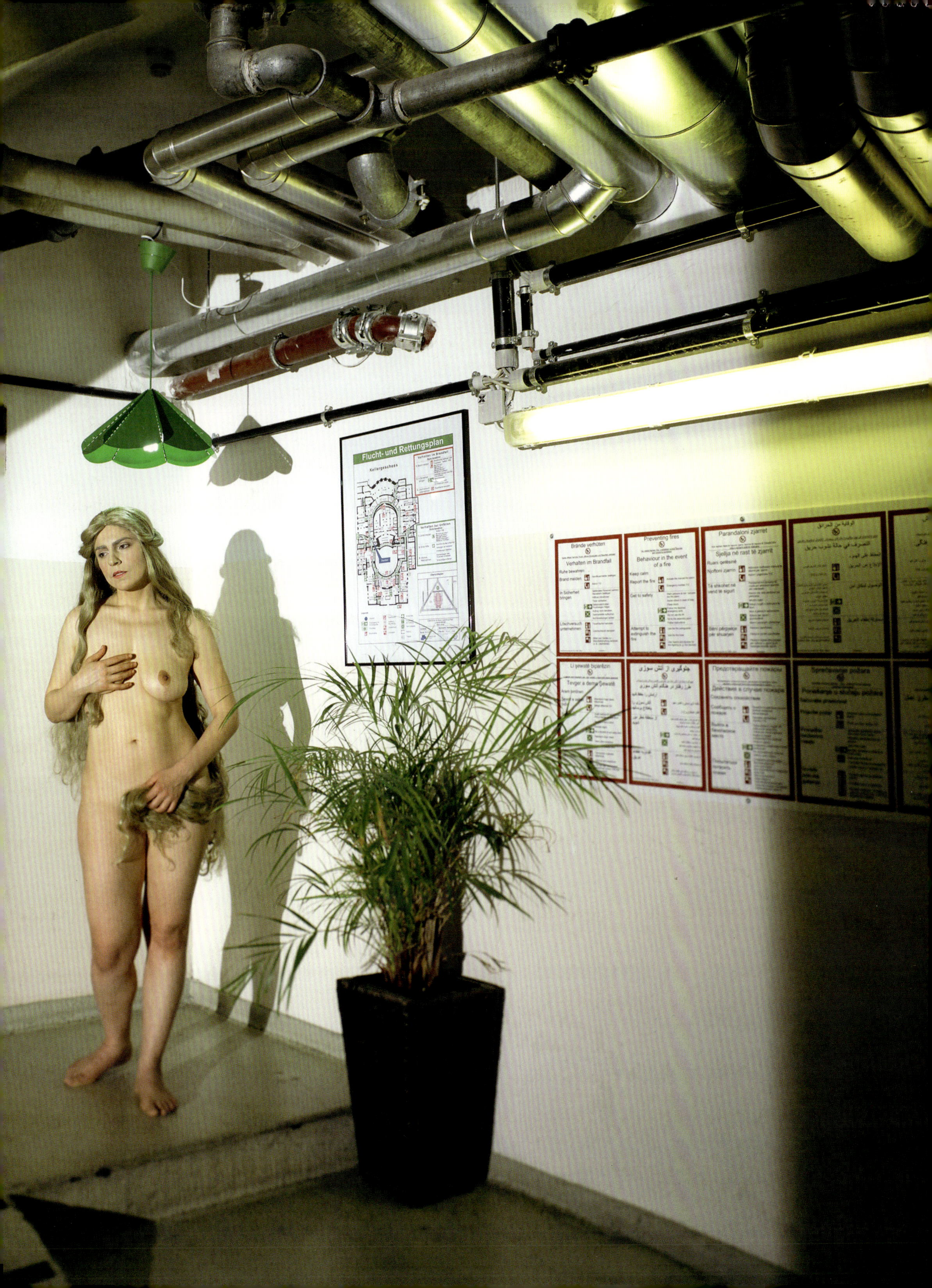

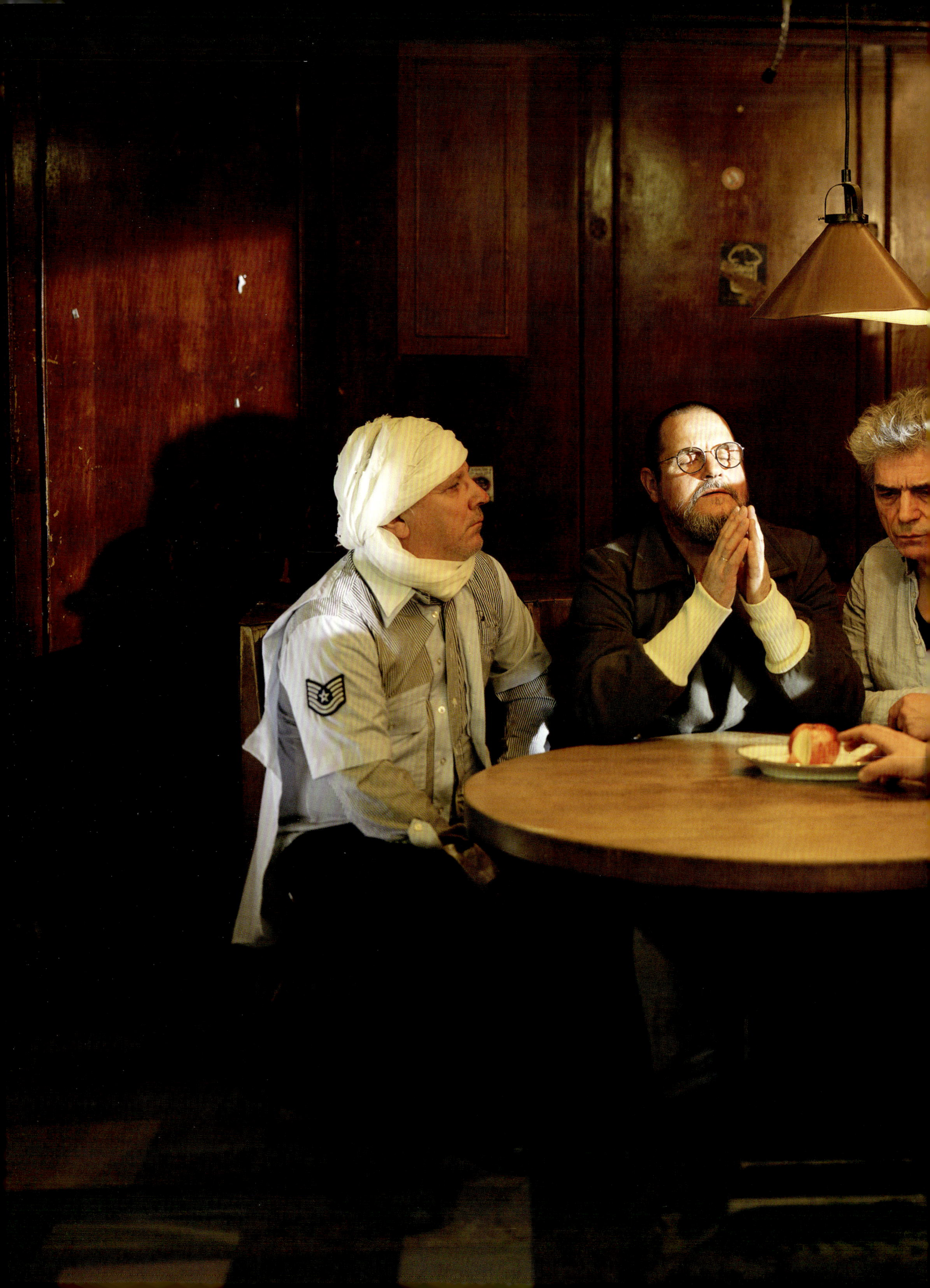

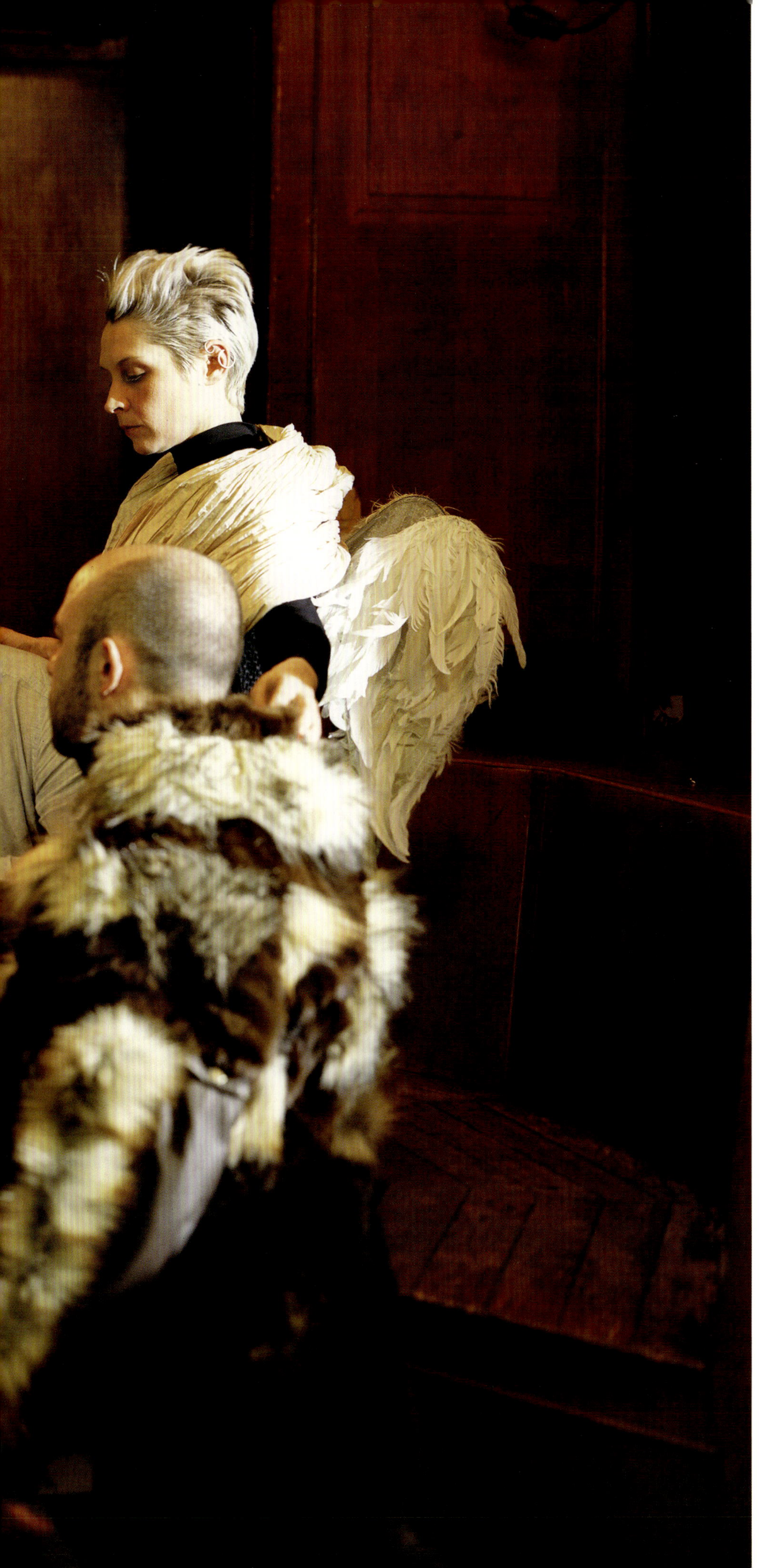

Andreas Speichert, Frank Mittmann
Jörg Wilkendorf, Ann Christin Müller
Konrad Walkow
The Healing of Tobias – Caravaggio
Tom Hunter, 2019

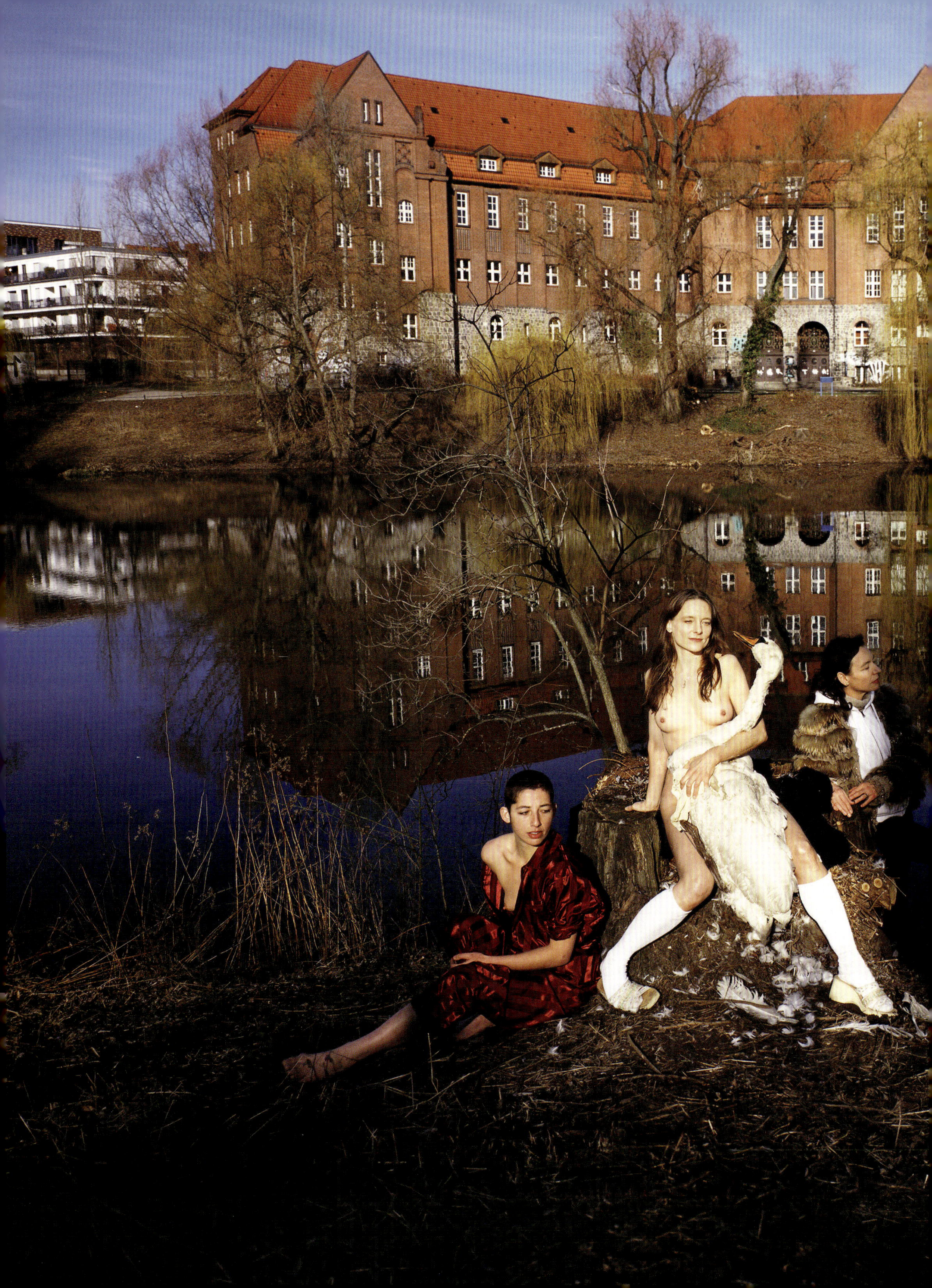

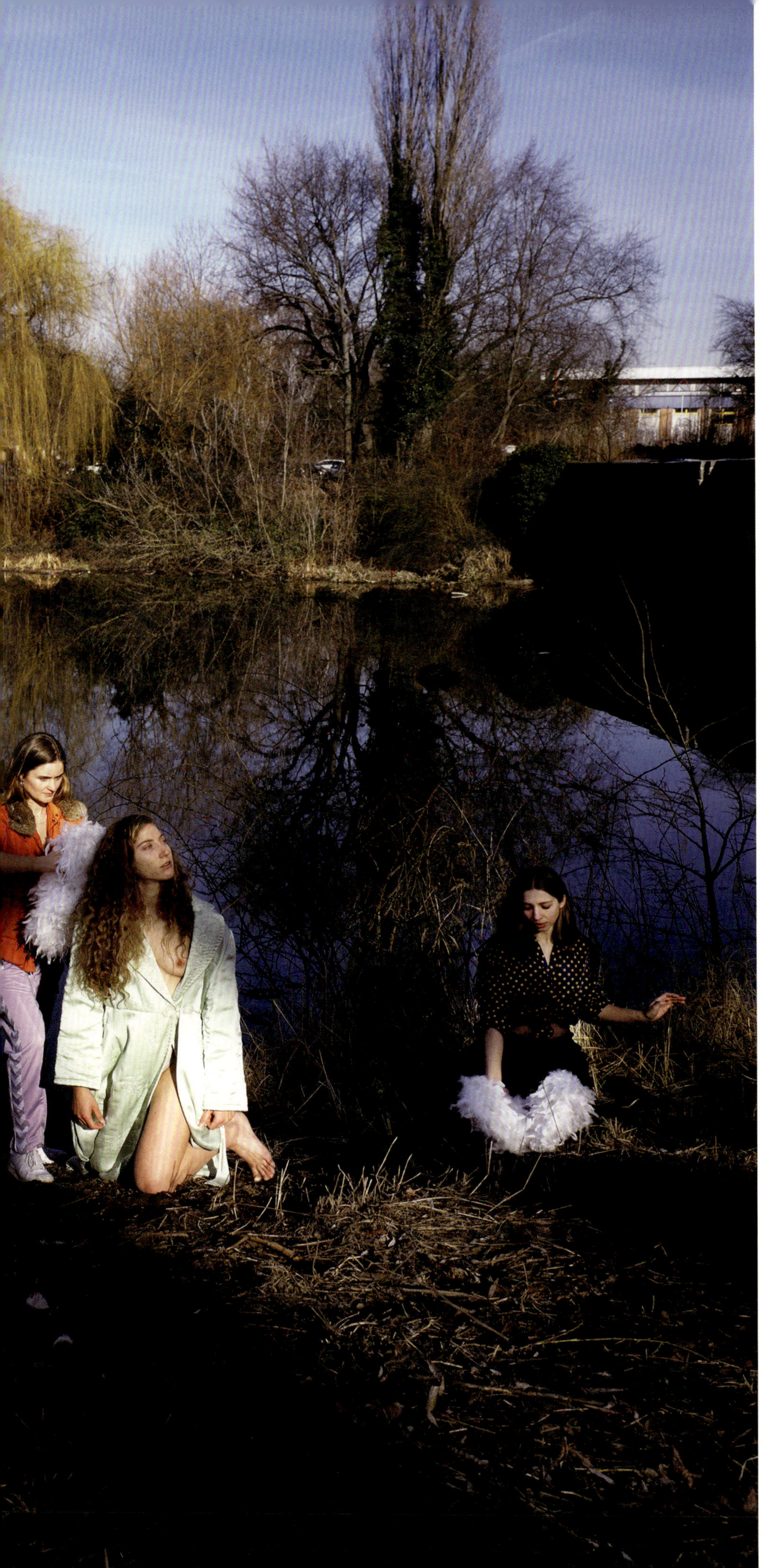

Eli Cohen, Anne Ratte-Polle
Ulrike Köhler, Eleonore Carrière
Alisa Golomzina, Almog Kidron
Leda mit dem Schwan
– Antonio Allegri
Tom Hunter, 2019

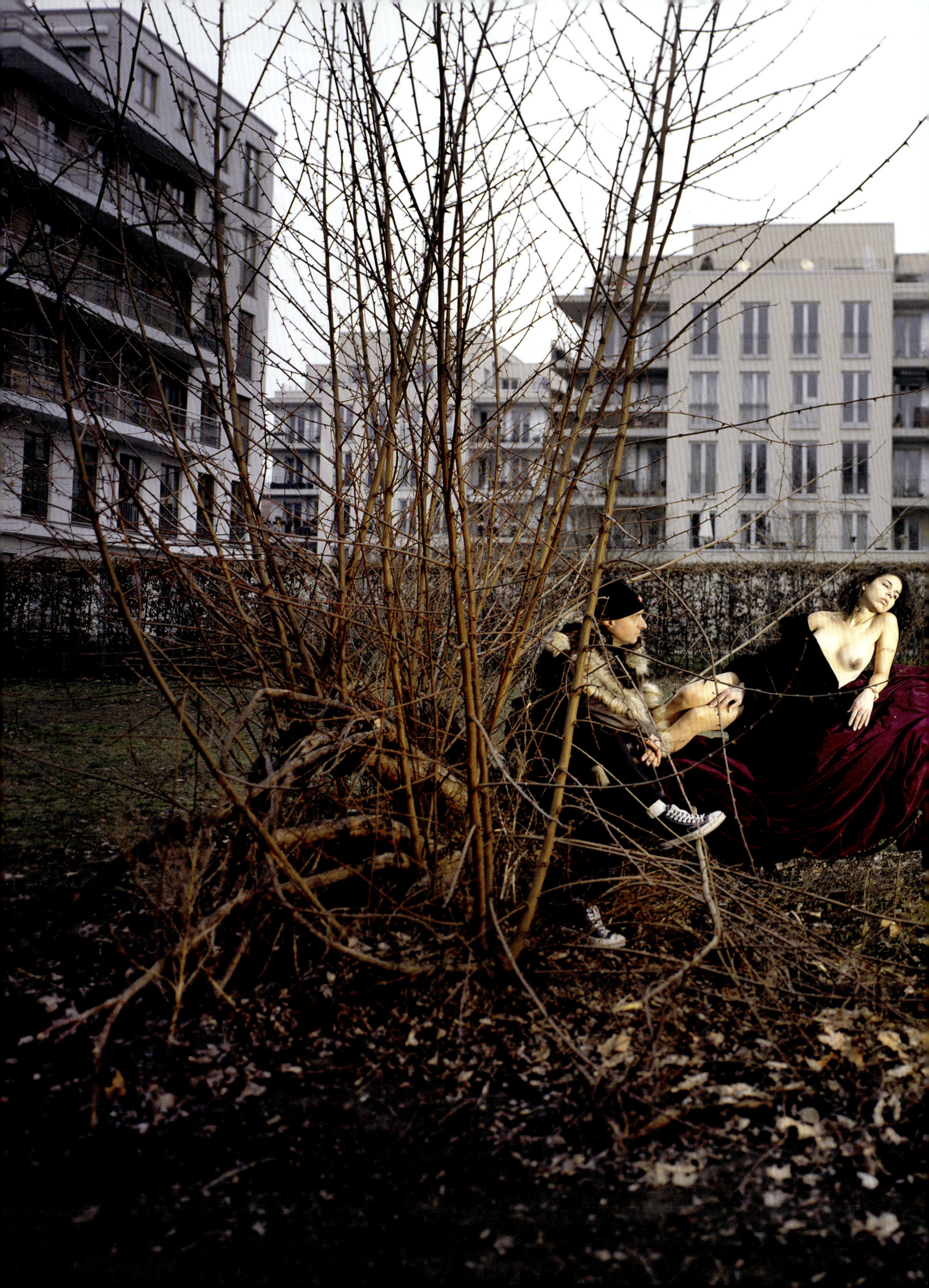

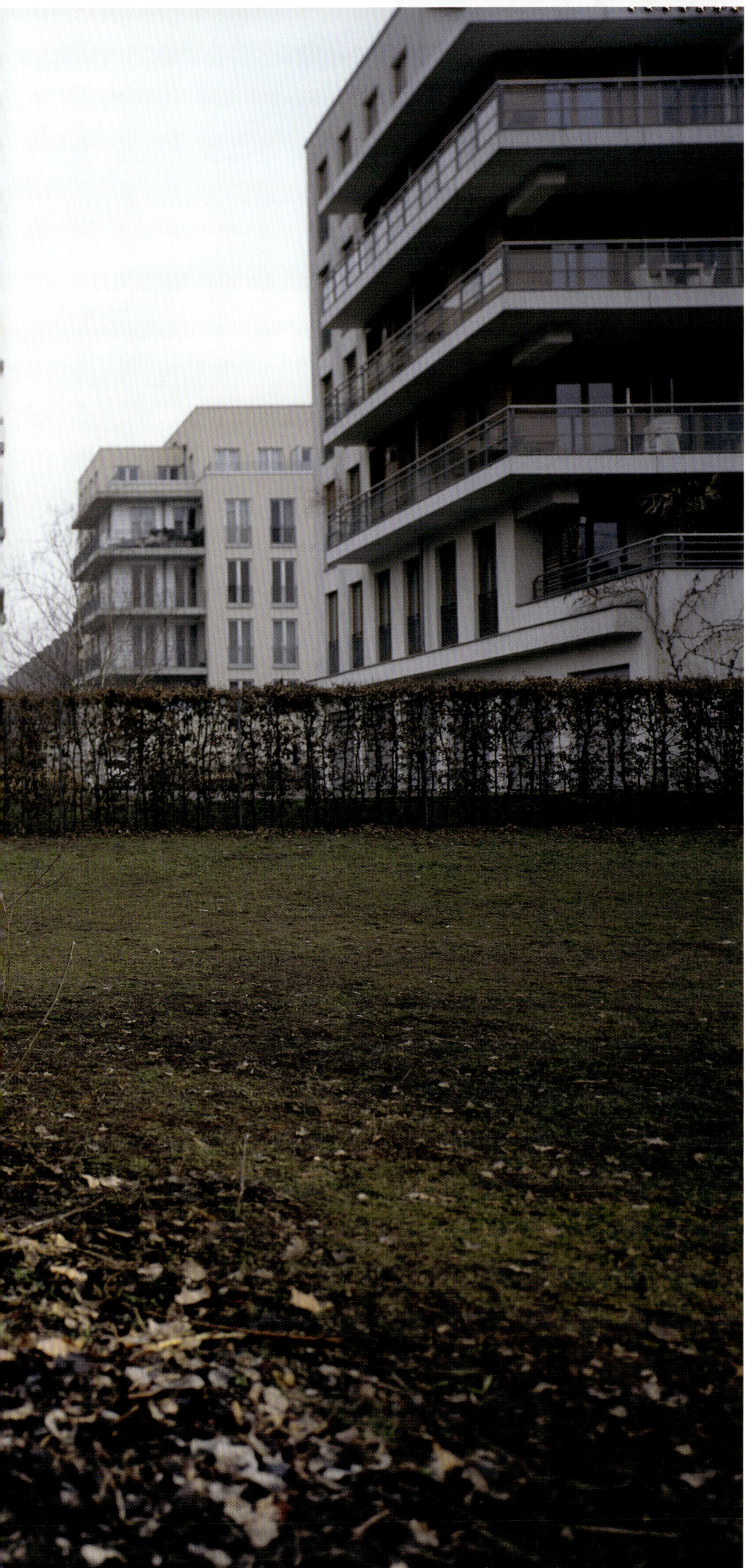

Manuel Osterholt
Sanni Marie Cabral da Silva Neto
Venus mit dem Orgelspieler
– Tiziano Vecellio
Tom Hunter, 2019

Leander Dörr, Eric Kyun Woong Kim Garcia,
Sebastian Bark, Niklas Draeger, Bruno Mathes
Die Fußwaschung Christi – Dirck van Baburen
Tom Hunter, 2019

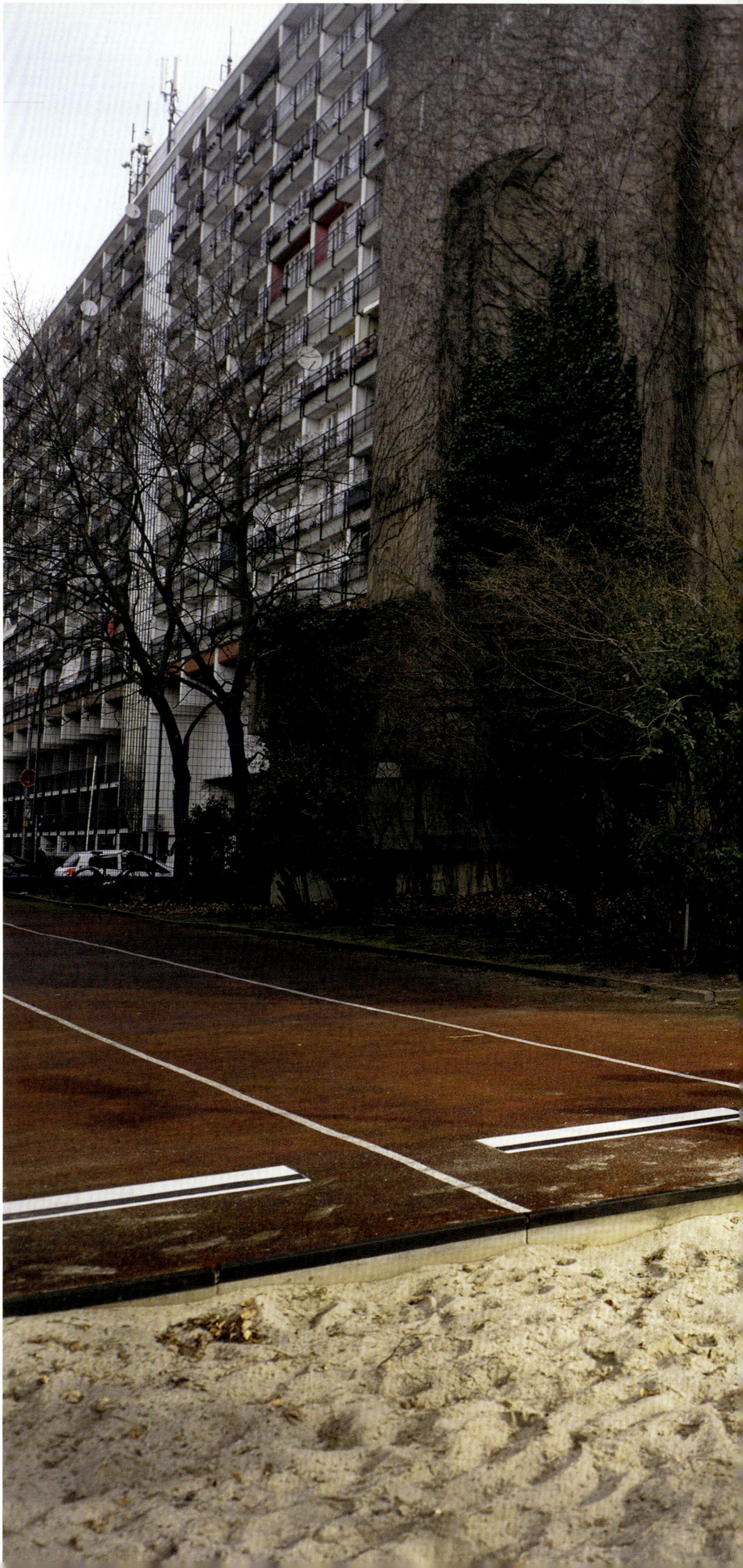

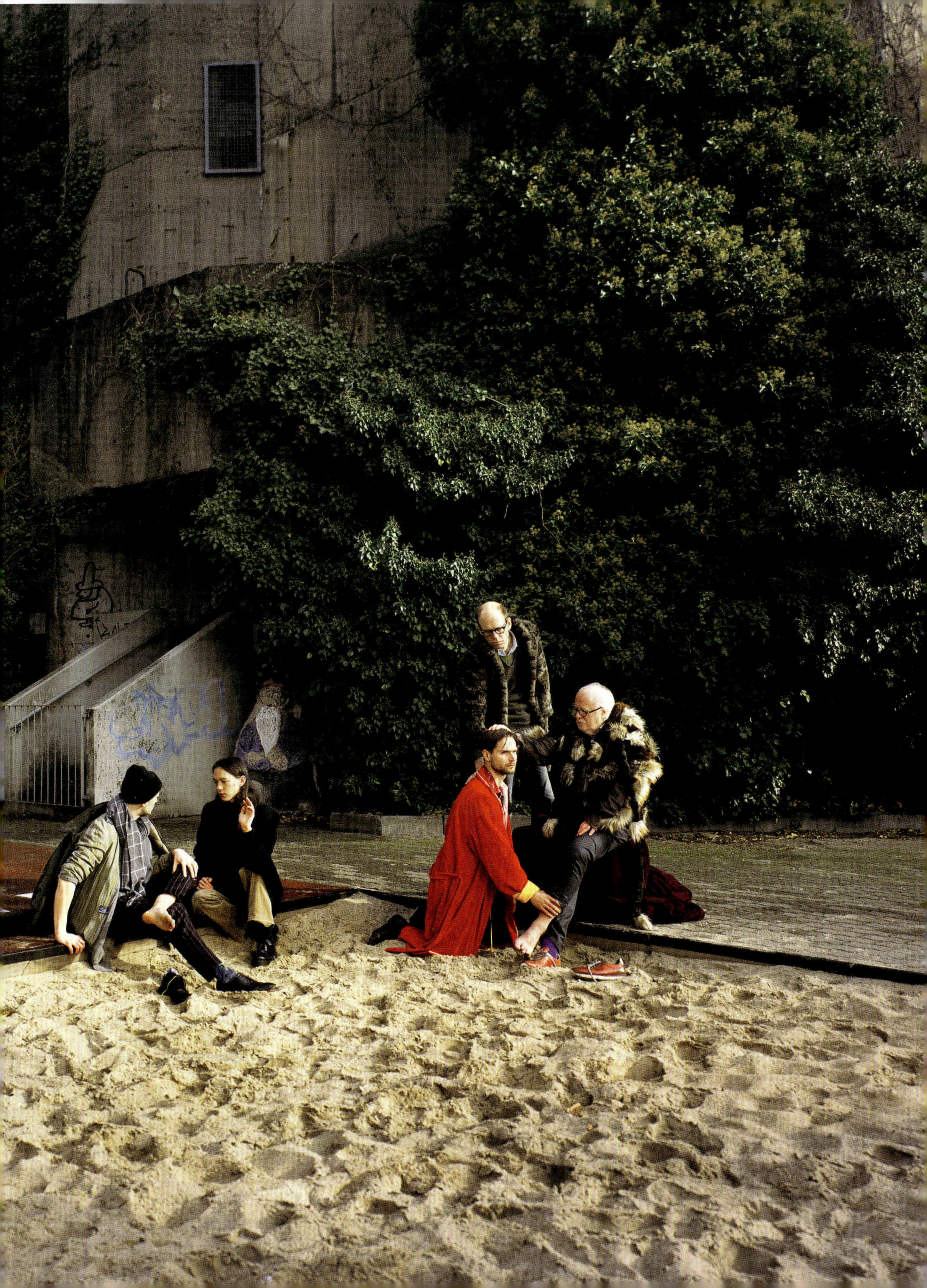

Thomas Schuller, Roland Naumann,
Elias Geissler, Eike Grögel
Das Abendmahl – Leonardo da Vinci
Tom Hunter, 2019

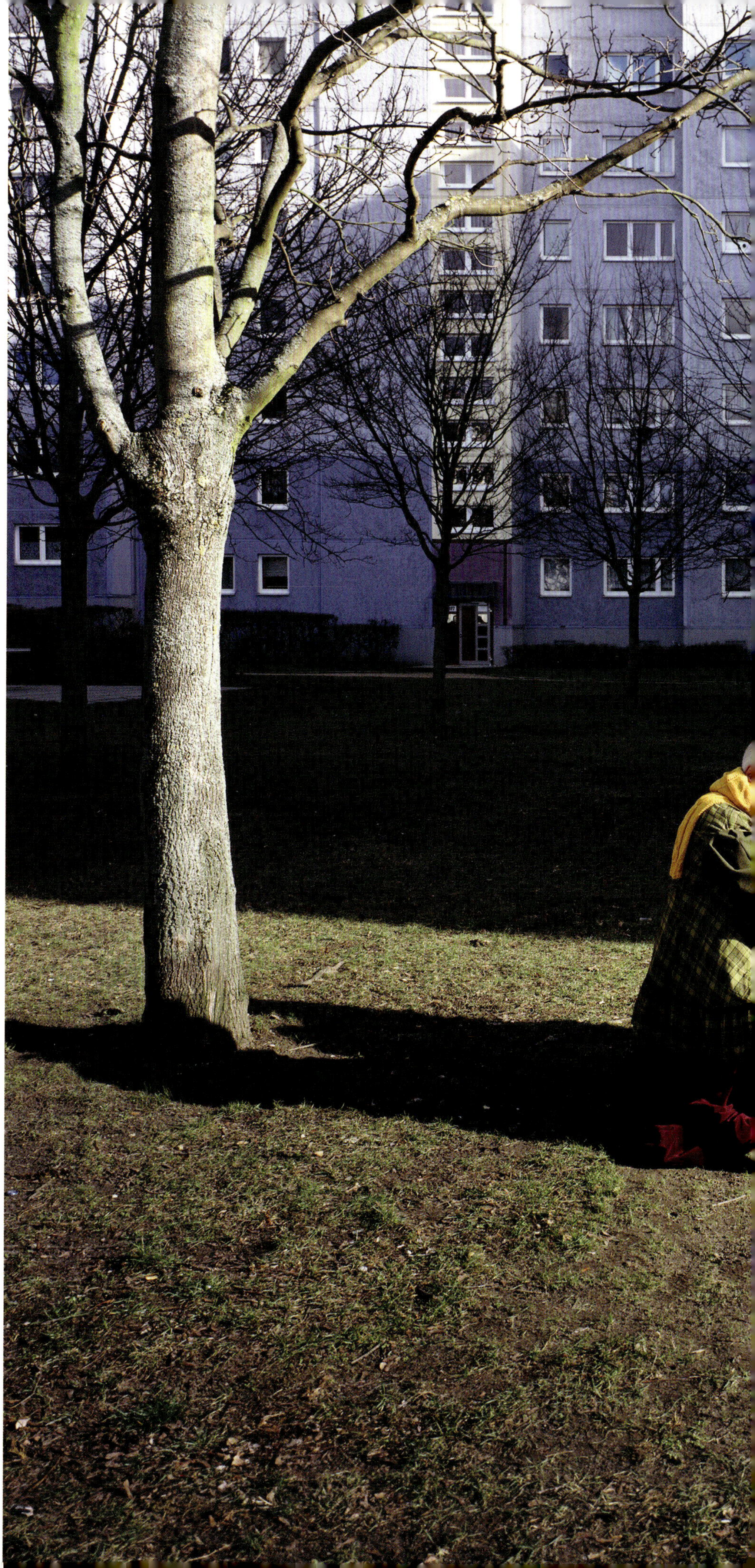

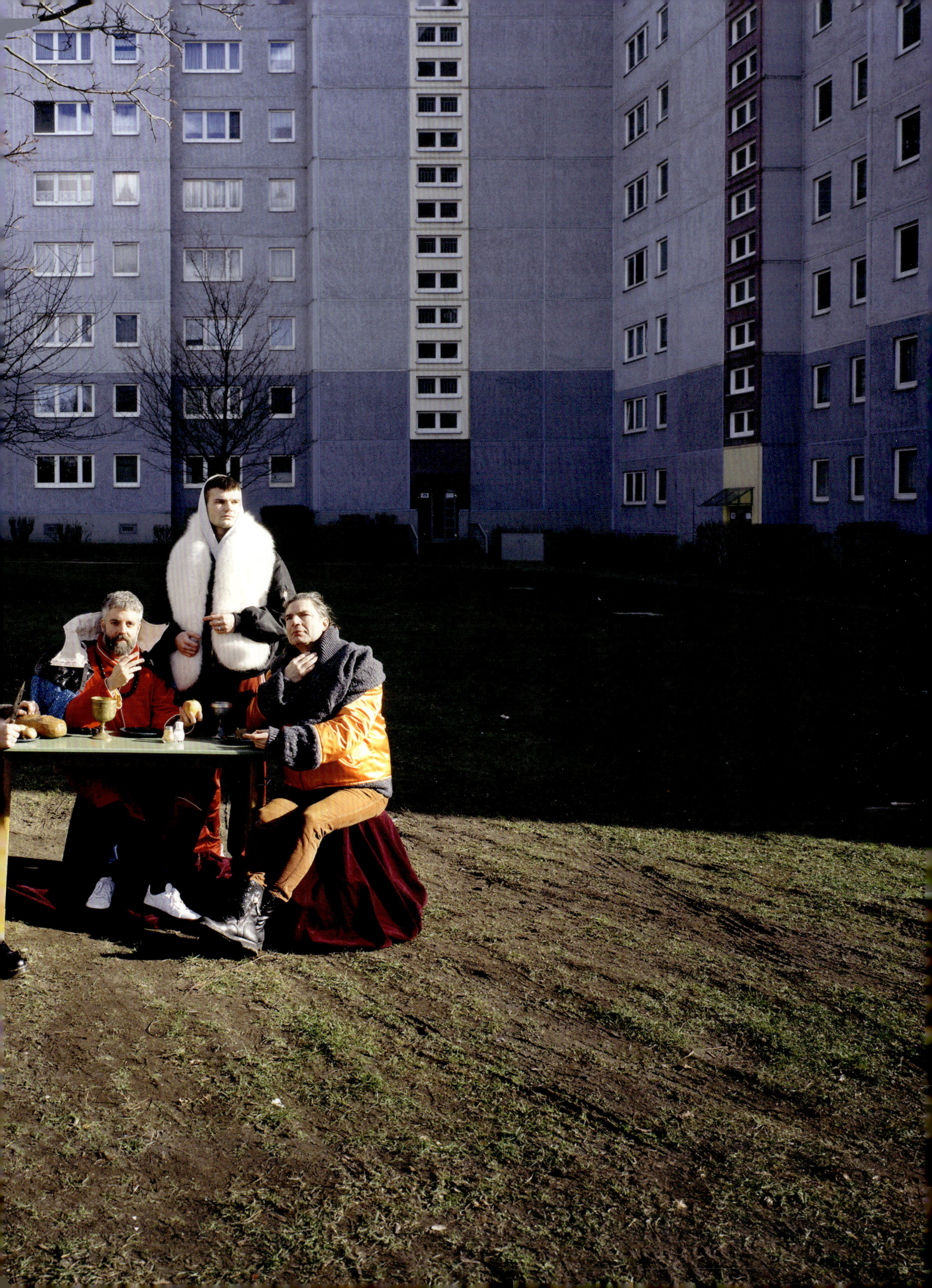

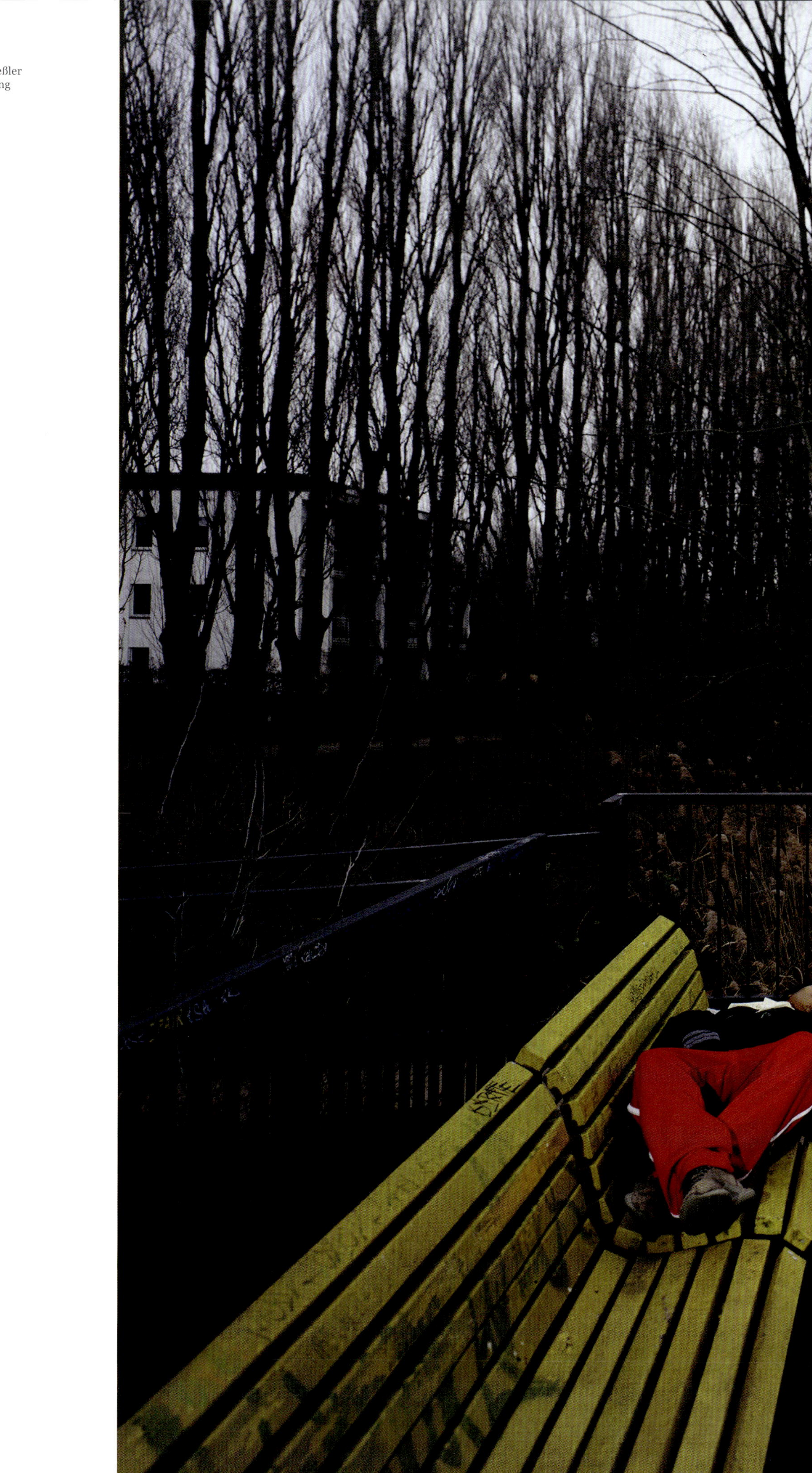

Thulani Lord Mgidi , Margherita Keßler
Pyramus und Thisbe – Hans Baldung
Tom Hunter, 2019

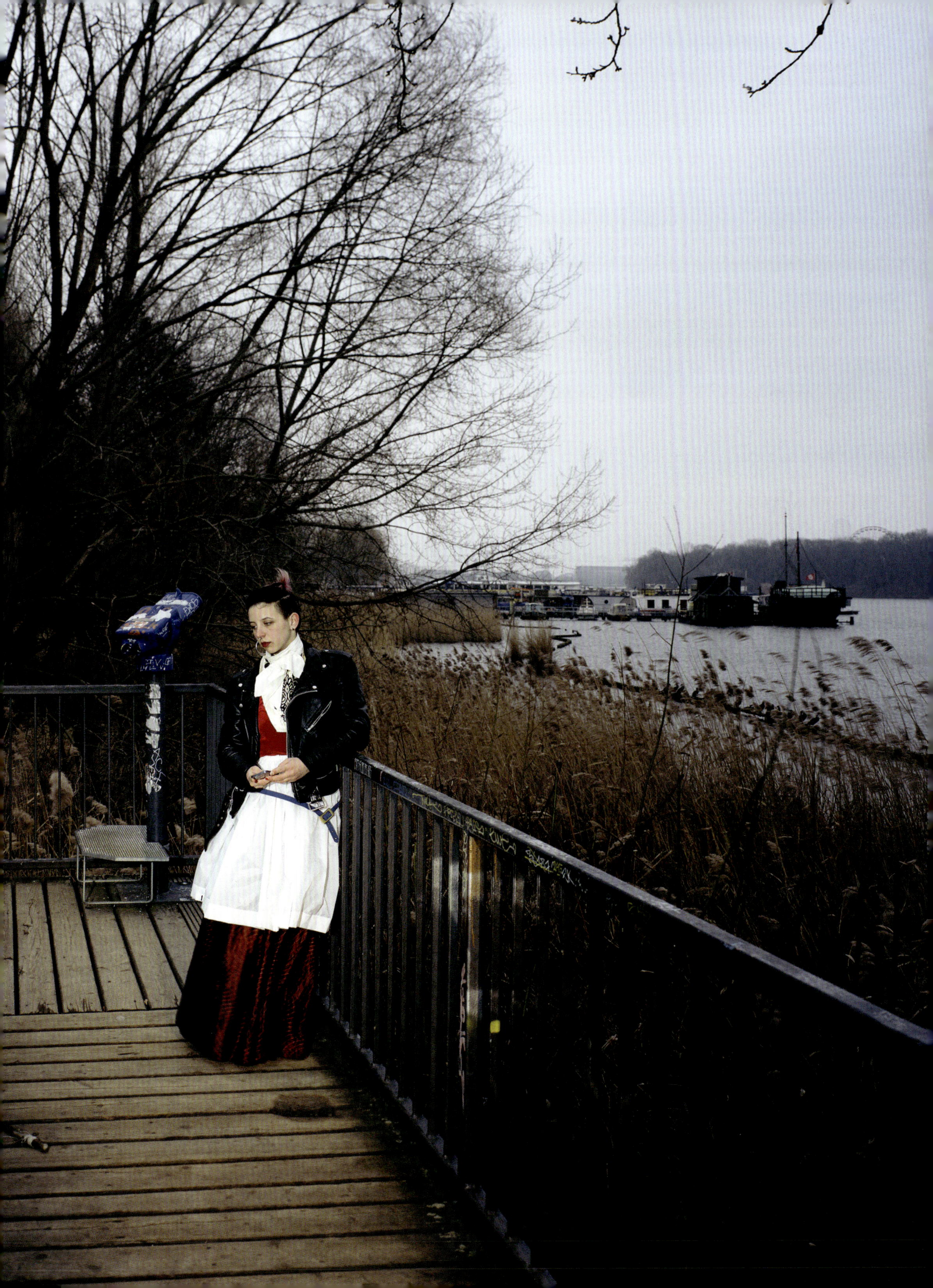

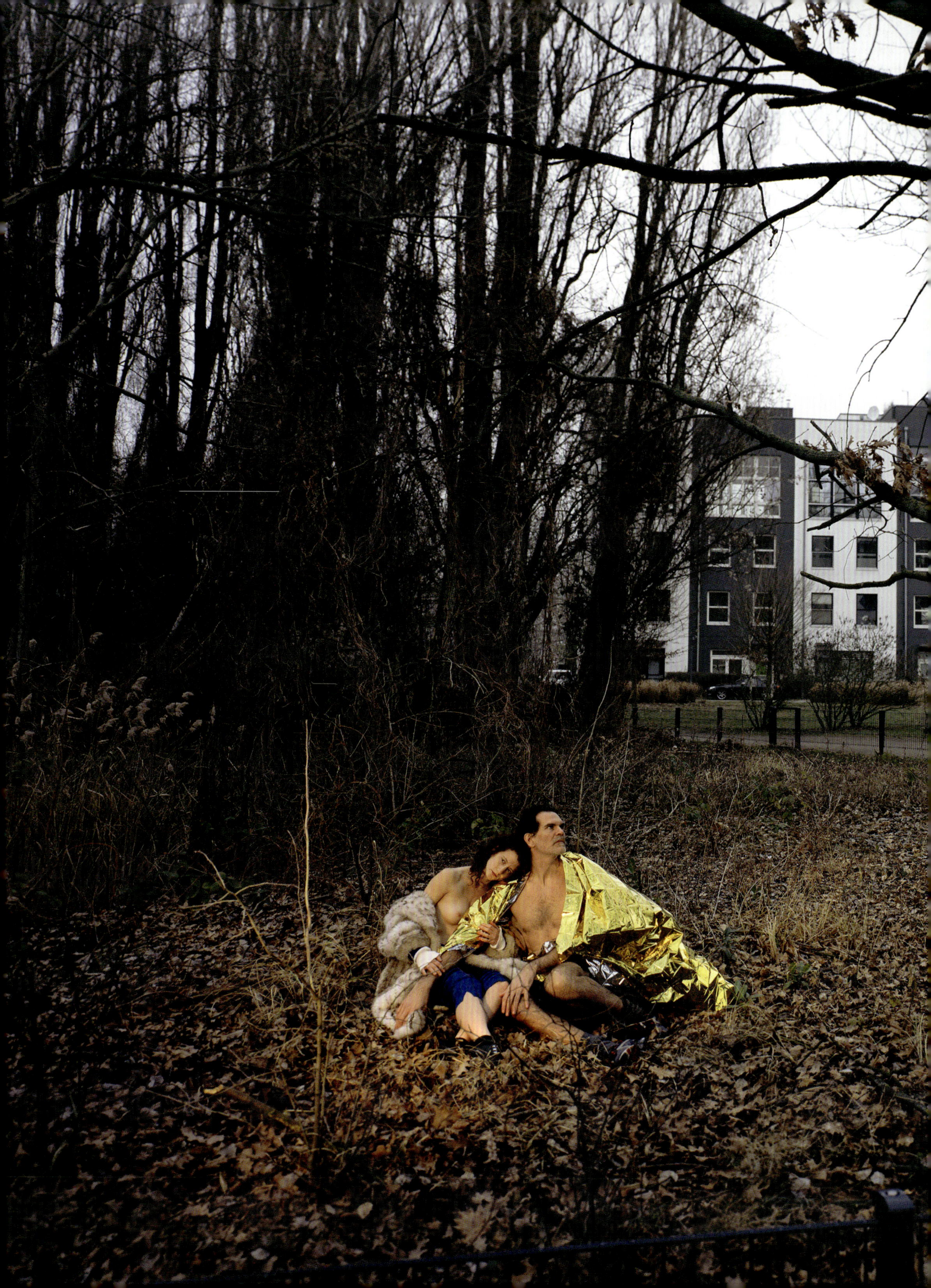

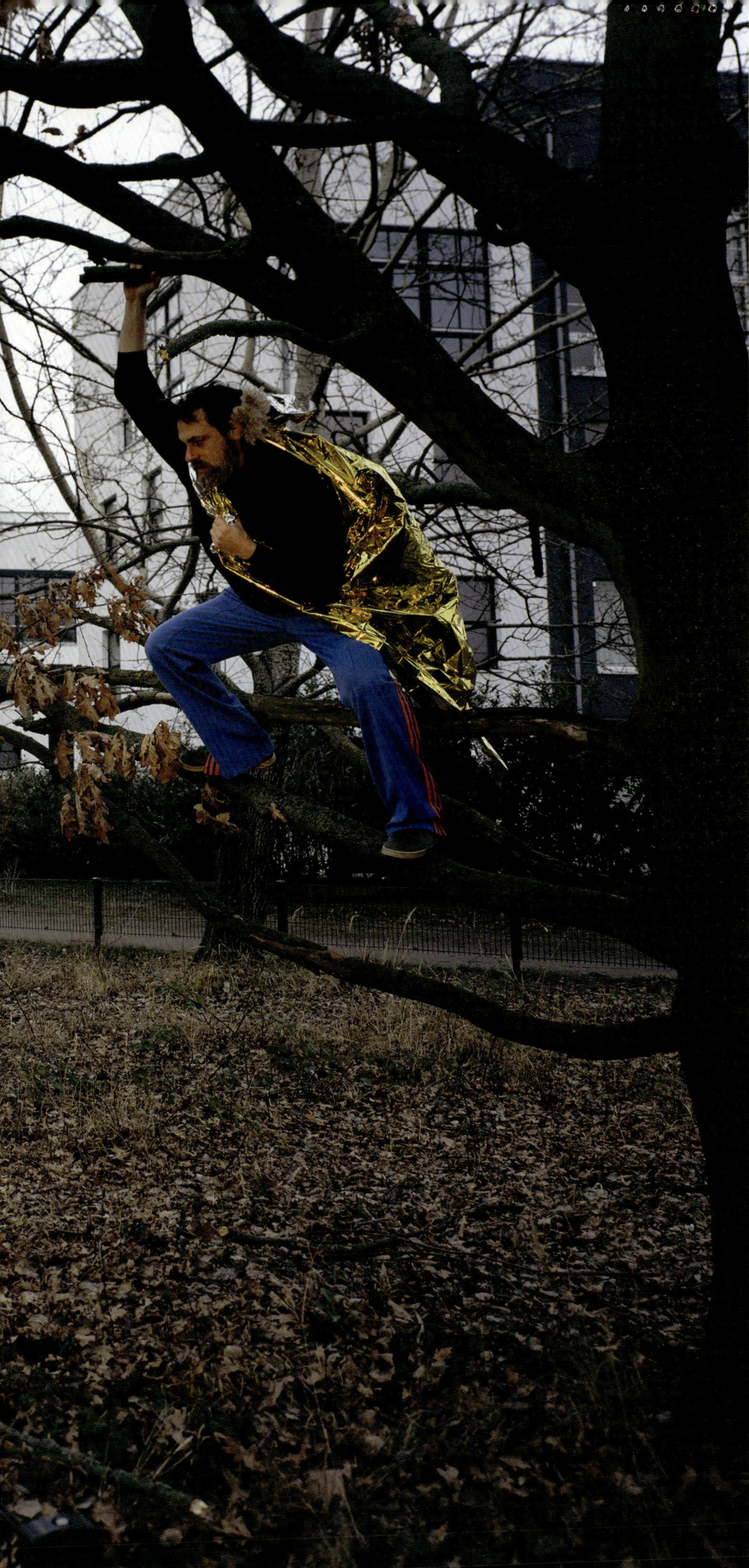

Adaya Berkovich, Luc Guiol, Santiago Blaum
Mars und Venus von Vulkan überrascht
– Paris Bordon
Tom Hunter, 2019

GRAPPLING WITH GENTRIFICATION

by Poligonal

Christian Haid and Lukas Staudinger from Poligonal in conversation with
Laura Calbet Elias, Nihad El-Kayed and Sandra Oehy.
Excerpts from interviews and e-mail correspondences, October 2022

The term gentrification was coined by the British sociologist Ruth Glass in the 1960s to describe a particular process of transformation in inner-city neighbourhoods: the displacement of low-income residents by a higher-status clientele with more income. Gentry, the term used to describe the lower aristocracy, was given its name because Glass drew parallels between the transformation of London in the 1960s and the city's developments in the 18th century, when the aristocracy moved from the countryside into the city and displaced the less well-off urban population. Since the 1960s, the meaning of the term has evolved with the increasing complexity of urban transformation processes, and the long-held narrative of a process that turns low-income areas into affluent trendy neighbourhoods has largely become obsolete because it falls short. What is needed is a differentiated view that takes into account a multitude of local and global actors and their interests and that replaces the linearity of earlier explanatory models. Gentrification processes are multicausal and multilocal. They have to be seen in the context of global neo-liberalisation, migration, financialisation of the housing market and the dissolution of the binary urban-rural logic. Thus, the discussion about gentrification is a conflictual debate that should be discussed across disciplines and leads to the question of which understanding of gentrification is germane in 2022. How do these processes affect the everyday lives of residents? How can urban policy counteract them?

We asked three experts: *Laura Calbet Elias* (LCE), an urban researcher working on the financialisation of the housing market; *Nihad El- Kayed* (NEK), an urban sociologist with a research focus on the changes of neighbourhoods through migration since 2015; and *Sandra Oehy* (SO), an architectural theorist, art scholar and exhibition maker.

In urban research, we distinguish between two types of transformation processes that condition gentrification: cultural processes and economic processes. Cultural processes mean changes on the demand side, while economic processes influence the supply side. Society has changed culturally: People have more flexible working hours, and for many the detached house on the outskirts of town is no longer desirable. Living models are therefore increasingly city-centre oriented: this leads to increasing demand in the inner cities and thus to the gentrification of these areas. – LCE

Gentrification often begins with the search for the „authentic". So-called „gentrifiers", often from different subcultures and intellectual, cultural milieus, seek and find this in urban spaces that are still little commercialised. Through their arrival and, to a certain extent, their violent cultural appropriation of the existing context, they change these spaces. When the subsequent commercialisation eventually leads to the McDonaldisation of neighbourhoods once characterised by, for example, traditional Arabic snack bars, this is usually rejected by the gentrifiers in their search for folkloric authenticity. A well-known example is the McDonalds in Berlin's Wrangelkiez, which opened to great protest. – SO

On the economic side, on the other hand, we see devaluation and appreciation mechanisms on the real estate market as gentrification drivers and speak of a discrepancy between yield expectations and what one actually gets for a property. According to Neil Smith, one of the pioneers of gentrification research, gentrification and the associated displacement occur when owners upgrade the building fabric or the use of a property in order to achieve higher profits. In the German discussion, culturalist explanatory models have dominated for a long time. However, gentrification is increasingly understood as multicausal - i.e. the joint consideration of economic and cultural factors. – LCE

It can be seen that gentrification processes particularly affect marginalised groups. In migrant neighbourhoods, there are many clubs, shops, restaurants and institutions that offer multilingual services. Such neighbourhoods are often places where information about jobs or vacant flats is informally exchanged and contacts are made. Former residents who have moved away from these neighbourhoods, either voluntarily or by force, often like to come back to visit friends, shop or eat out. In the process of gentrification, the price of housing rises, as do commercial rents. If at some point the rents for these shops, restaurants, associations and initiatives become too high, these places lose their function as urban resource pools and as hubs for networks, exchange and as places of arrival for new migrants. Refugees who have come to Berlin since 2015 have often been housed in migrant neighbourhoods where they would usually find good connections. However, due to the gentrification of recent years, there is hardly any chance of finding a flat there. Many only find one on the outskirts of the city (if they do at all), where racist discrimination is unfortunately more common. – NEK

With the arrival of financially stronger clientele, the use of the urban outdoor space often changes. The newly arrived residents' desired sense of security moves to the fore. This is expressed, for example, in the increased use of hostile architecture, which, for example, makes it impossible for homeless people to spend the night on park benches and similar structures, and often also in an expansion of street and park lighting and the disappearance of dark niches. Various existing uses of public space are thus prevented, and the socially weaker are pushed out of the urban space. The priority of a neighborhood's public space is for clean and quiet use so as not to reduce property values. Extremely gentrified neighbourhoods often also appear increasingly generic and sterile in aesthetic terms. – SO

The critique of gentrification is not about preventing upgrading but about regulating housing policy and decommodifying the housing infrastructure. However, this approach does not come from politics but mostly from social and civil society movements:
Examples are the rent referendum, the referendum on the development of the Tempelhofer Feld in Berlin and the Initiative Deutsche Wohnen und Co enteignen, as well we also initiatives for a new real estate policy and a new tenancy law at the state level. At the political level, the term gentrification has only recently become very widespread. City governments and administrative apparatuses have questioned gentrification as a concept for a long time and only belatedly realised that there is an acute need for action. Recognised researchers like Andrej Holm have been warning about the gentrification spreading like a snail throughout the centre of Berlin for about 20 years. However, urban policy has still taken time to acknowledge these developments and discuss measures. In 2022, however, we are at a point where political forces have changed again, and the old housing policy is resurgent, demanding liberalisation at all levels and thus marking a turn from a progressive and fairer housing policy. But the last word has not been spoken: There is still a lot of potential for political movement. – LCE

On the topic of housing policy, it is worth looking at other European cities. A very common and successful model in Vienna and Zurich is that of social housing and cooperative housing. Planning by housing cooperatives often manages to counteract some of the negative effects of gentrification. These projects are mostly created from the beginning for a mix of different social and socio-economic classes and family models. In some cases, parts of the private space are also made public, which adds value for the residents of the surrounding neighbourhood. The problem with this model is that capital must already be contributed at the beginning. So despite the inclusive approach, not everyone can afford this. It would therefore be desirable to push for public urban housing that follows a cooperative mixed model. Policymakers could encourage this by setting a quota for cooperative and social housing, as is already the case in Zurich, for example, through a referendum. – SO

In addition to the major rent policy initiatives from Berlin civil society such as Initiative Deutsche Wohnen & Co enteignen, there are approaches in the thematic field of migration and housing that attempt to support marginalised groups in their search for housing. These include, for example, counselling centres that explain how to look for a flat and give tips on what documents are needed and how best to put them together. Discrimination against people with names that do not sound German is also on the rise in an increasingly competitive housing market. In this regard, more and more approaches are being developed to help reduce discrimination (e.g. by the Berliner Fachstelle gegen Diskriminierung auf dem Wohnungsmarkt). These are important developments, but given that rents are rising rapidly - and thus housing market discrimination is becoming easier for landlords - they are effectively a drop in the ocean. – NEK

We should also reflect on whether gentrification is still the appropriate term: It can be argued that the effects of gentrification do not only mean displacement in the housing market, but also lead to lower purchasing power. In connection with inflation and rising energy costs, the question therefore arises: How much can people from lower social classes actually continue to restrict themselves? Someone who has already been watching every penny for the last few years has no further possibilities to save. The number of those who depend on food banks and free food distribution points is increasing rapidly. We are heading towards a situation where, because of the high costs of housing and energy, it is also a question of whether people can still afford food. So if the housing issue in one of the richest countries in the world is really linked to the hunger issue, then we have to think about what kind of society we live in and how much of the welfare state is actually left. In the current energy-saving linked to the war in the Ukraine, political ideas are also coming to the table that, interestingly enough, we know from the debate about housing. Maybe the difficult situation in 2022 will finally open our eyes as a society that regulating vital infrastructures like housing is not the wrong thing to do. – LCE

TESTIMONIALS

Portraits

I have been living in a Wagenplatz (trailer park) for several years. Since I became a father, my life changed and I couldn't spend so much money on living in an apartment. There are about 20 of us living in this Wagenplatz community. Many of my neighbors have been leading this lifestyle for a long time, some of them were even born here. Everyone owns a trailer but we have an additional communal car, as well. Once a month we have a plenum where we discuss neighborhood issues.

Life at a Wagenplatz is quite nice: simple but cheap and still central. You only win with it! Of course, apartments are nice and comfortable, but this lifestyle also means high rental costs and you have to somehow obtain the money. This causes lots of struggle. Wagenplatz's way of life enables you to take a break from time to time, to say „I worked a lot last month, now I can take some time off". Here you have a great combination of quietness and urban life. On the one hand, it is very quiet here, on the other hand you can reach Kreuzberg in 10 minutes by bike. It is not very far, a few U-Bahn stations and you are at Kottbusser Tor.

Unfortunately, already since the start of this year we have no lease, because the owner refuses to renew it. We asked for an extension until the end of this year, and have only recently gotten a provisional six month extension.

We do not know what exactly the plans are with this real estate. Rumors indicate that there is a housing development in the works, but we know neither its precise status nor whether investors have a building permit and financing. We suspect that we just have to go preemptively. The property is simply worth a lot more and attracts more buyers without residents – I mean, without us.

What will happen? It is impossible to know. But I am sure of one thing at least: the city is changing a lot. I was born here, Berlin has always felt very easy. Finding an apartment wasn't a particular problem. Finding a job wasn't particularly problematic either. It might not have been a large sum of money, but you didn't need that much either. That sort of lifestyle completely vanished in the last ten years: everything is subjected to commercialism. And the social structure that represented many of us, the places we liked, the affordable Kneipen, all these are disappearing, step by step.

– Daniel

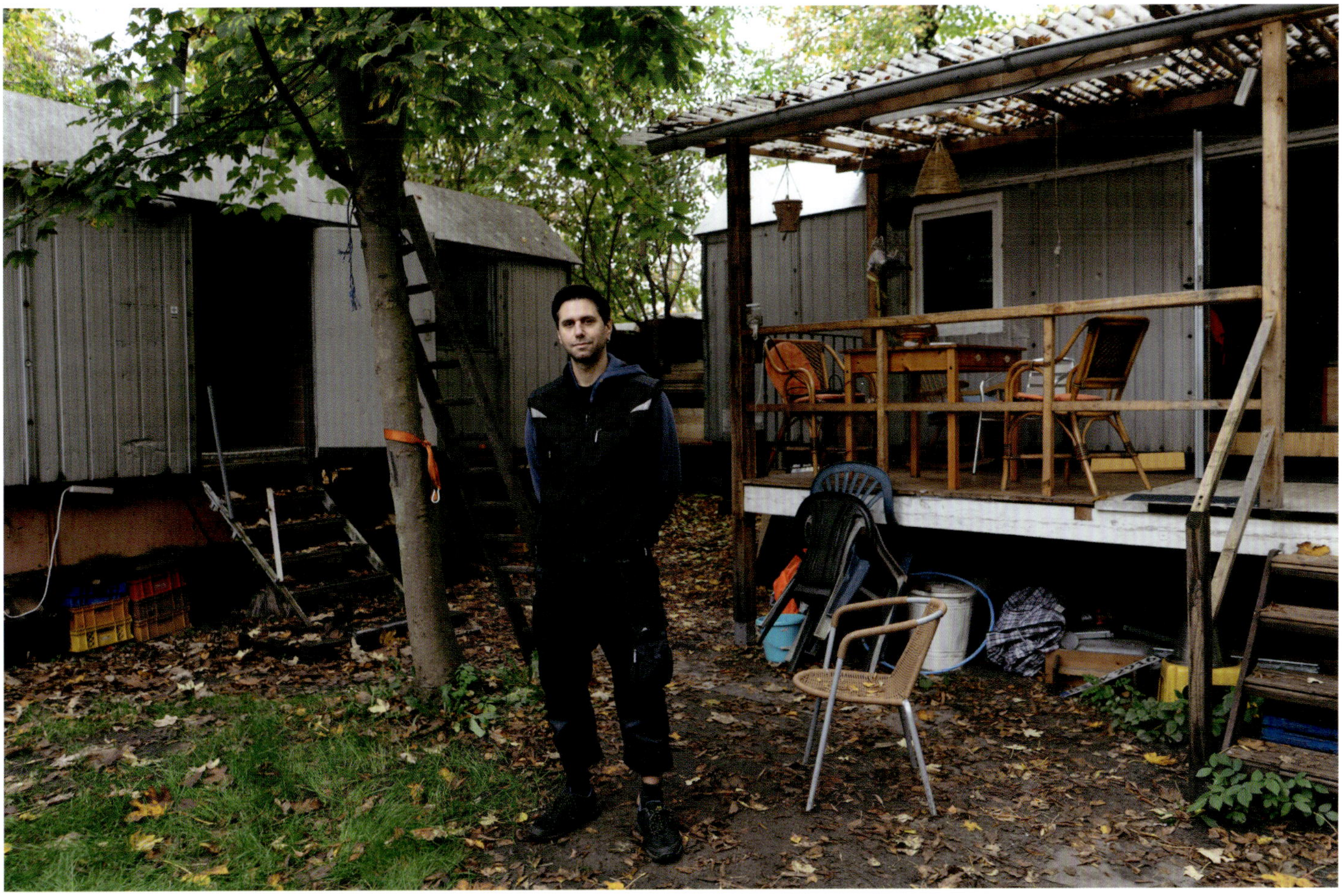

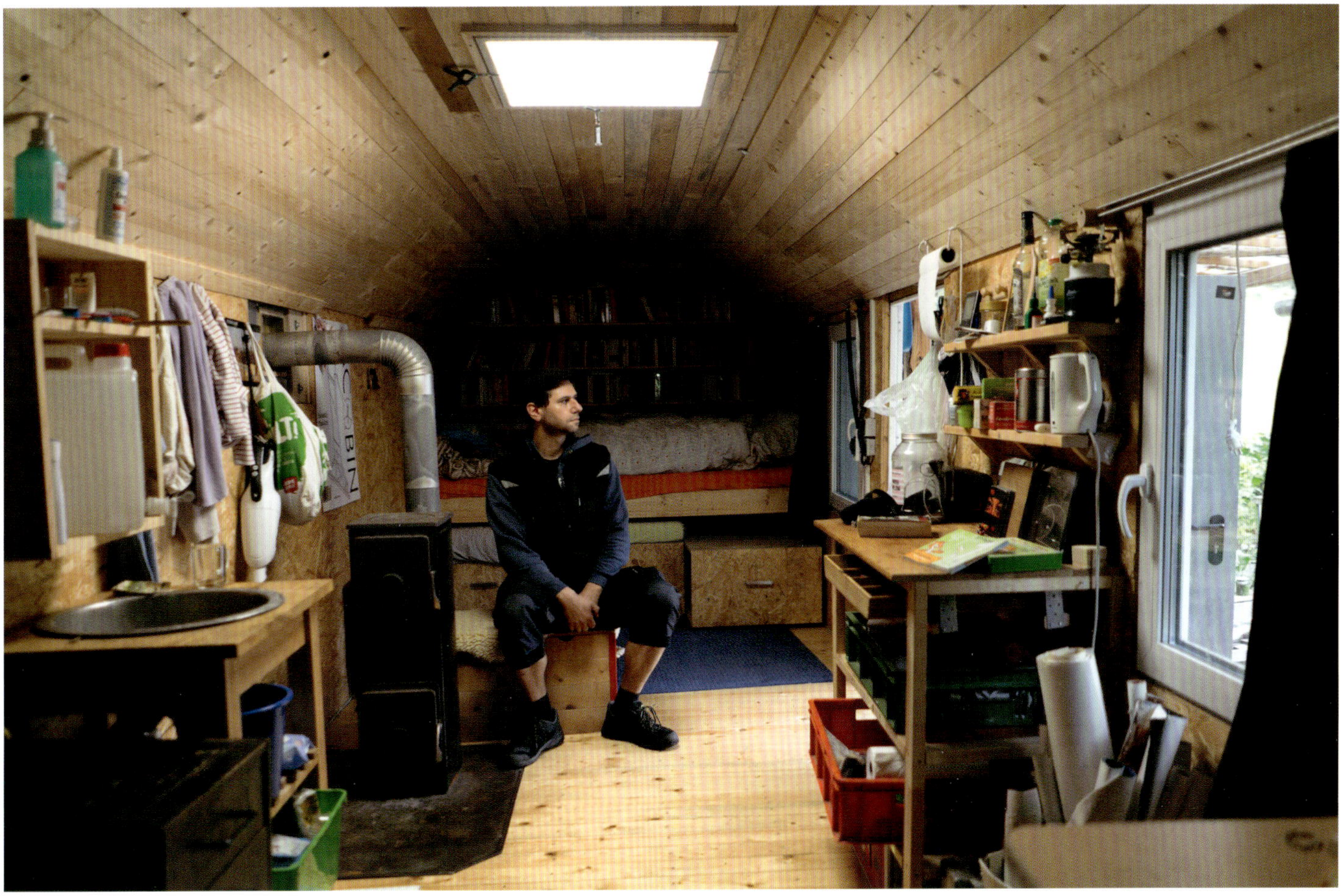

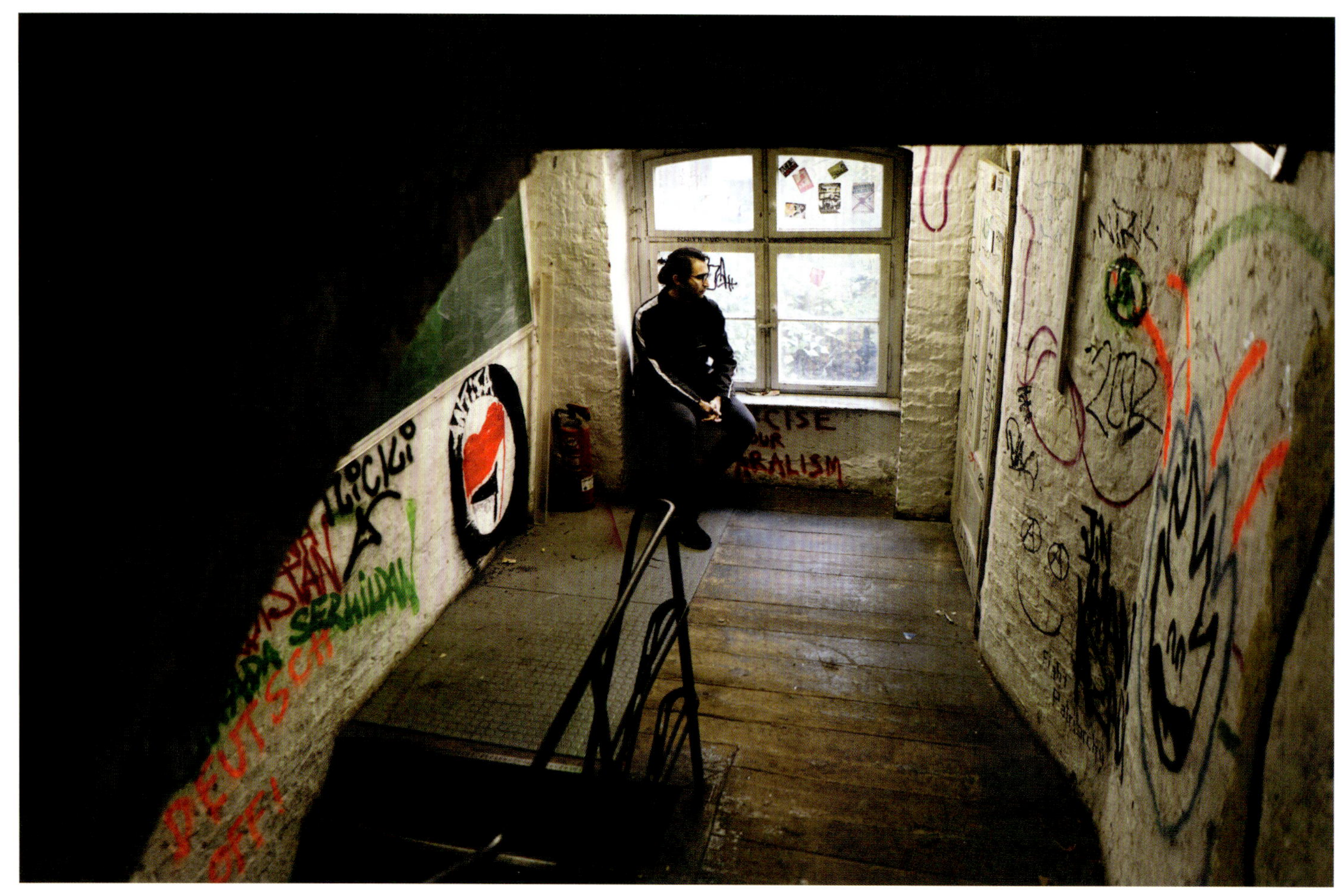

I moved to Berlin more than five years ago. Since the beginning of 2018, I started living in one of the many collective self-organized house projects that Berlin has. I left the house a few months ago because I moved out of the city, but I am very grateful to have made a pass through there: I learned a lot about sharing sources, sharing space and building a way of life based on solidarity in a capitalist society.

We were around 50 people living there, so you can imagine: the house we lived in is huge. Straight people, trans and other queer people. Arabs, Latinos, and of course, Germans too —you know, these kinds of projects are impossible to survive -from a bureaucratic point at least, without Germans or "people with privileges" in Germany!

What is interesting about a project like this is that you get so close to other people who are different from you gender-wise, language-wise, culture-wise, economically-wise. You share common spaces with workers, artists or students. This of course has pros and cons, but I would say that you learn a lot about other people and their struggles. In the meantime you see how racism works, identity politics and police brutality.

The problem started a couple of years ago. The owner of the house doesn't want to renew the renting contract. And he wants to evict us arguing, among other reasons, that we were using the house for our own benefits, subletting the rooms to make a money difference, which is totally not true. Why does he want people out? It is not difficult to guess his motives. Doing some quick math, you can see: with the whole gentrification in the neighborhood for example, you can get at least twice as much money than we are paying today for our rent.

I am not sure what is going to happen, the legal process is ongoing. But the option of winning seems less likely. In case that the of eviction option wins -and even before, people always need to keep thinking of "creative" ways to reclaim their city and their space.

– Ali

I moved to Berlin in 1998 and started to live in this WG (shared apartment) where I still live with a roommate. Sigmund, the owner of our house, who also owned 20 or 30 other apartments in this housing complex, lived next door. He was actually born here. Initially, the relationship with him was very friendly and easy going.

Five or four years after we moved here, Sarah, my roommate, who was the primary tenant on the contract (Hauptmieterin), decided to leave the house. She suggested signing a contract over to me and another member of the WG. To be honest, at that time I thought that Sarah was being kind of crazy. Why did she want so much formality? Anyway, I signed. Sigmund signed the contract too. Life went on, time passed. Years later, a new Hausverwaltung was appointed to manage the property. And that was the first moment where I saw it clearly: things were changing.

A representative of the new house services made an appointment to come and see me. He asked me to show him the house contract originally signed and the later transfer - the Nachvertrag. Then he said: "It looks like none of the people living in this house are legally here, except for you. The best that you can hope for is that you are the only person who can stay here". I was very surprised! So I called the Mieterschutzverein, a tenants' ombudsman's office, where they helped me understand the situation. They told me clearly: "The owner of the house lives in the same house and can see all what's happening, so don't leave, you are not doing anything wrong".

From that point onwards, life started to get difficult for me. I had to declare every new person coming in and out of the WG and the Hausverwaltung started to reject some people.
Some time after, they accused me of deliberately damaging the infrastructure of the house, installed a special device in the bathroom which monitored the humidity of the air and accused me of having furniture that was damaging the floor. For each accusation, I had to write a letter in response, proving that this was not the case.

At some point I understood the reasons for this harassment and wrote a letter to the owner. In other words, my proposal was: "Let's try to negotiate something, I understand that you are sitting in a goldmine and you want to make more money, so maybe we can find a solution. For example, every time somebody moves in, we can make a rent increase". I didn't get a reply to this email. In the late summer of the same year, I woke up and I got a very aggressive knock on the door. Three policemen were standing in front of my apartment. They were accompanied by Sigmund. They came into the house, went to my balcony and found six marijuana plants growing there. They took the plants away. The next day, Sigmund came with a yellow envelope containing an eviction letter.

So then the court case began. Two and a half years after – with a pandemic in between– I won. Justice proved me right, I could stay. But the whole situation was not without cost to me. I started to have severe panic attacks. I always took for granted that I was safe in my home, and realizing that this was not like this was annoying. However, I plan to stay here, not without a bittersweet feeling. I am living with an inexorable certainty: this place does not belong to me.

– Marcus

GARTENFELD ISLAND DEVELOPMENT

Interview with Thomas Bestgen

On Gartenfeld Island in Berlin-Spandau, UTB is working with municipal, cooperative and private developers to build a new sustainable neighborhood on more than 37 hectares with around 3,700 apartments. Is the Gartenfeld a model project for innovative, social and sustainable urban development? Is it intended to serve as a good practice example for future urban development? A talk between Constanza Macras and the founder of UTB Thomas Bestgen about this project - and an excuse to think, from this model case, about other possible ways of constructing and living.

Constanza Macras: How did you bring the project of Gartenfeld to life?

Thomas Bestgen: Gartenfeld was previously an extremely polluted industrial area. The whole housing crisis, but also the crisis of urban development, turned into a challenge for us to transform small urban quarters, which we have already developed in the last 20 years, into something of considerably larger dimensions.

I was very happy to accept this challenge, the development of the whole city district now on this island, without great consideration of already outdated technologies or obsolete infrastructures – for example: car friendly but not people friendly mobility structures. Our goal is to develop a district that is more than just a residence.

Our approach based on solidarity has played a major part in this. That is, those who can afford more invest more and those who cannot afford it get subsidized. The municipal housing sector, coops that are involved and the cultural sector paid significantly less to get into this project than the sector for high-end housing and for condominiums. We are an interdependent society and we have a social market economy. We are increasingly seeing how social structures that were believed to be secure are collapsing. Our attitude and our approach are therefore based on taking all stakeholders in urban society with us to participate and we succeeded in doing so in Gartenfeld.

CM: These are, then, also projects in social housing?

TB: Exactly. We have almost 80 % of houses that will be for rent. That means that sponsors who are developing Gartenfeld have predominantly rental housing on offer. We therefore have a third of the area subject to rent control. As a result, the Gartenfeld – though a purely privately initiated project – has more social housing than in conventional projects and, above all, so-called middle class, which are known to be disappearing in Berlin and are increasingly losing access to affordable housing can also take part. We can therefore invite the entire spectrum of urban society to live in Gartenfeld.

CM: How can one build the city in a more inclusive and integrated manner?

TB: It is only possible through the cooperation of all socially relevant forces. This means that an equal footing must be established rather than determined exclusively by those who own the land and dominate over financial resources.

Private property is generally protected by our basic laws. But it is precisely here that the necessary balance is lost more and more due to the one-sided application of the concept of property because property also entails obligations. When the common view of social necessities is lost and individual interests play more and more of a role, there is a widening gap between those who have land and can develop the city and the actual needs of this city.

Of course, Berlin is somewhat unique. If one develops projects in Munich, Hamburg, or even

London, New York, Barcelona or Milan, that does not mean that it will work as well as it does in Berlin, or that it should work. At UTB, we try to have an overview of the needs of the city and its citizens.

For whom or what do we actually develop our projects? We don't try to generate finished product and above all we do not want it to degenerate into a product that is only about maximizing profits. Then the added value for the city would be lost and corporate returns dominate the development process and that can never be good, not even for investors.

As a result, trust is lost and this is how citizens' movements arise, which, for example, have the goal of nationalization and, for example, make their plight known through occupied structures. These are conditions that would not have been necessary if the interests of urban society had been dealt with earlier and more sustainably and, ultimately, their needs had been addressed more actively. We are therefore trying to better understand the needs of areas such as culture and society, to explore what is possible in dialogue and to incorporate them into urban planning. That's why we don't look at which house we can sell best, but how we can integrate the requirements and thus optimize the development.

Now that we are in a crisis of high interest rates, rising construction costs and skyrocketing land prices, only those developments that incorporate an inclusive and sustainable program will survive.

CM: What about sustainability? Is it also a concern for you?

TB: Actually, building destroys the natural environment, we do not have to delude ourselves about this fact. In Gartenfeld, we were dealing with already a quite highly contaminated industrial area that could not really be further destroyed by sustainable development.
Historically industry has contaminated the soil and the flooring. We had to answer the question of how to deal with it. Let's unseal everything, replace the soiland create more green space or do we use the existing space to open it up while building densely to create even more living space?

I think we've struck a good balance by completely eliminating soil pollution; that will provide a healthy living and working conditions. Besides, housing means more than simply the use of the residential space. Housing projects need to take into account also the neighborhood itself.

For us, not only sustainable building materials are in the foreground, but also a sustainable coexistence. Important topics are: energy, mobility, culture, green spaces, space for social issues and a city of short distances.

Due to global warming, for example, we must protect homes more and more from the effects of heat and develop buildings that react intelligently to the heat. At the same time, the winters in Berlin will remain cold, which means we work with intelligent systems that can do both in an energy-efficient manner.

This is where digitization helps us, algorithms can also be used to determine who is at home and when, then adjust the energy supply accordingly. If we know that only one in ten people are at home between 9 a.m. and 5 p.m., then we only need to produce ten percent of the energy. We have digital heat meters nowadays that know when hot water is usually needed: mainly mornings and evenings. This means that we can shut down the power plants and fill the storage facilities when energy is not being called up, so that it can be made available later.

CM: And finally, there is the question of mobility. What are your thoughts on that?

TB: Yes, transportation is another important topic. Berlin has been an incredibly car-friendly city. The paradigm of the federal government is still: no speed limit and expanding highways. That is completely misguided. We see that the new generations don't feel compelled to get a driver's license at all and even if they did, they don't see the necessity of actually owning a car. We are in fact providing a mobility-app in which all means of transport, whether car, scooter or cargo bike, are packed into one system. This will enable everyone to see in the morning which transportation options are available to him or her, how long it takes, how much it costs, and how many calories are burned.

What vehicle systems will be in use in the future? We will have to adapt to them as well. Gartenfeld is a blueprint for an integrated urban development. What is good for the environment and for the city is consequently good for people.

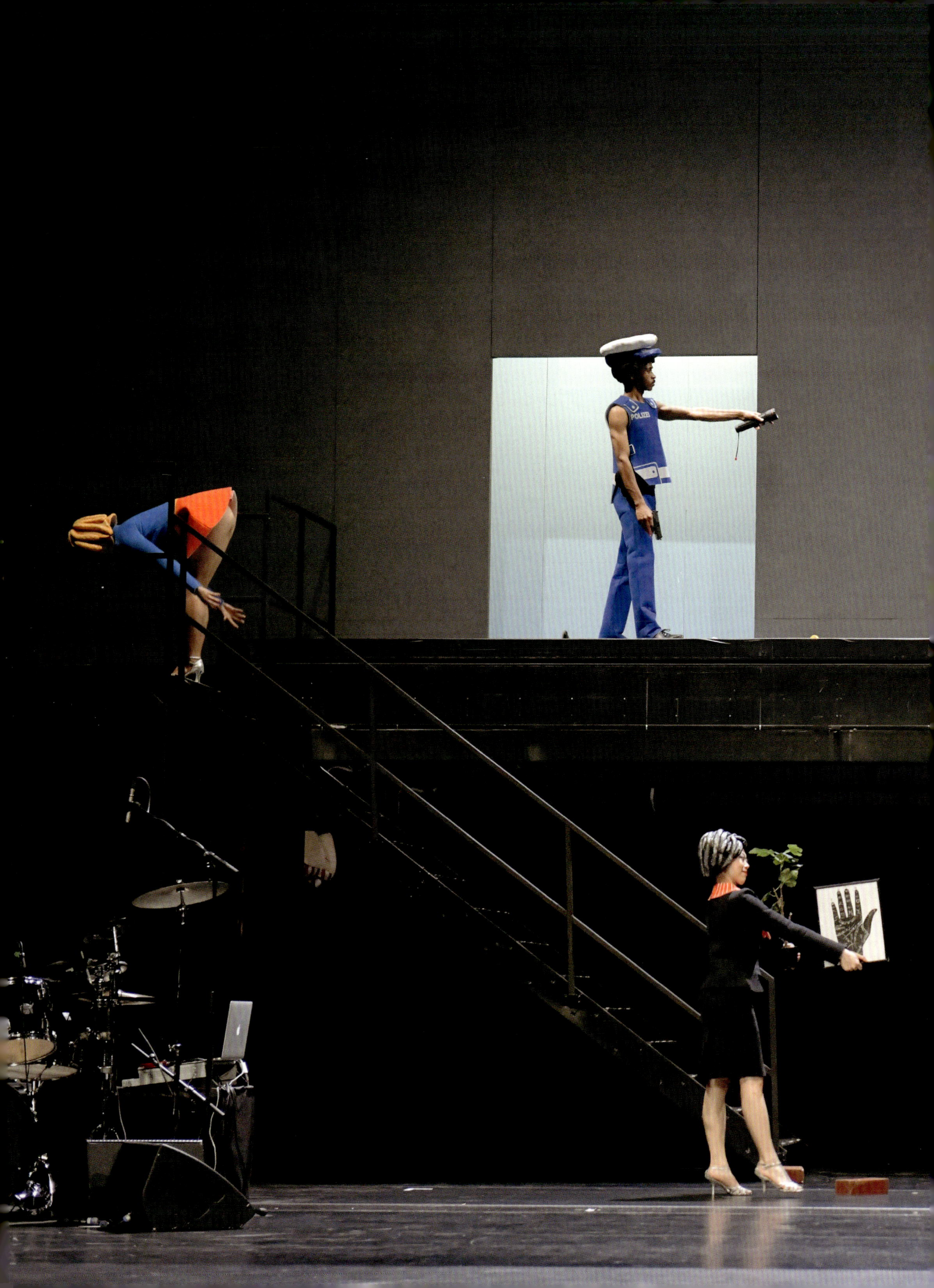

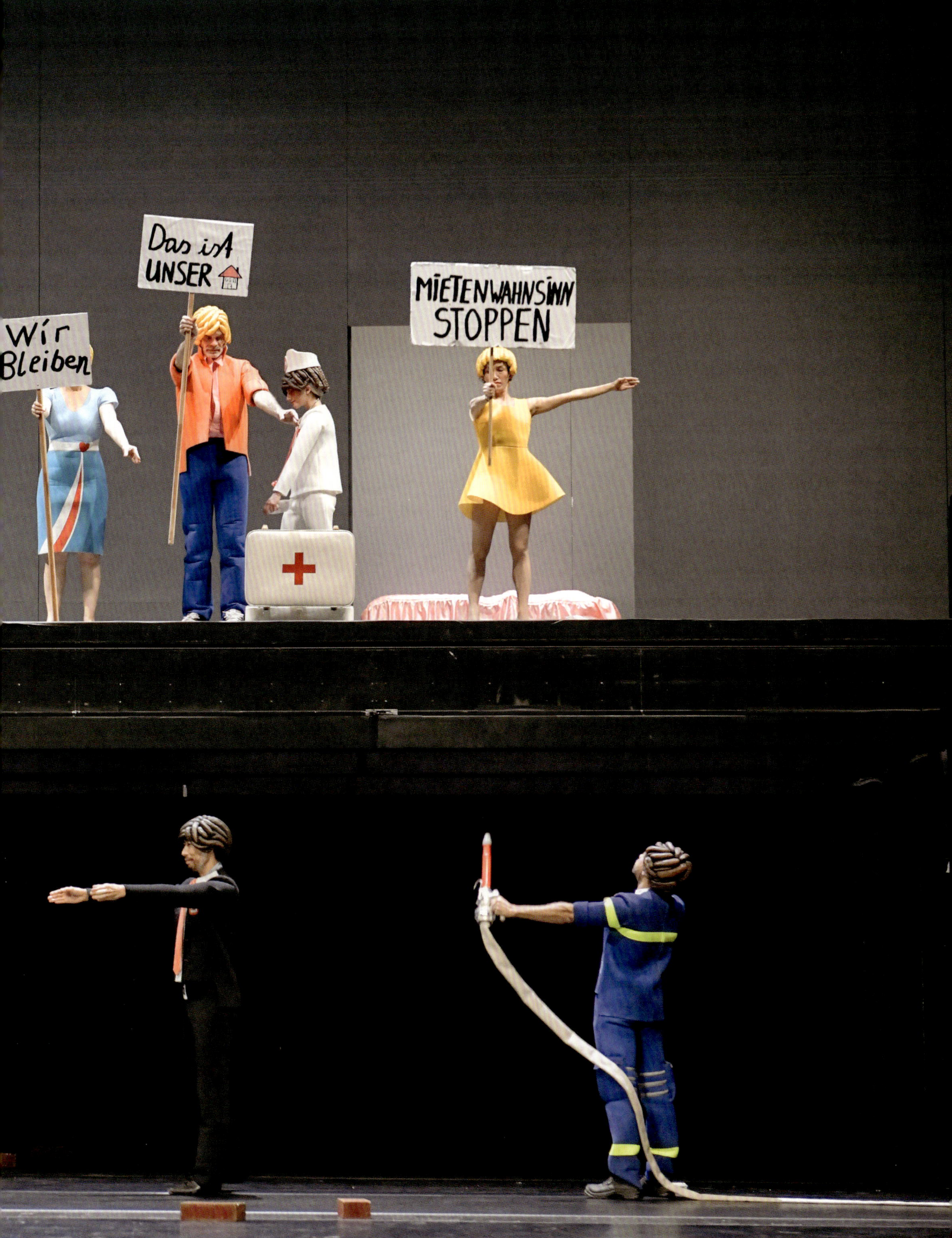
Wir
Bleiben
Das isA
UNSER
MIETENWAHNSiNN
STOPPEN

DANCING FOR A ROOF

by Natalia Laube

I am not ashamed to confess that when I went to see *Der Palast* I did so with the same secret presumptions I always have when I attend Constanza Macras' productions: that I am going to understand something more than the rest of the spectators sitting along beside me in the auditorium. I don't usually have the same smugness when I go to the theatre in Argentina – my native country, also that of Constanza – but, as a foreigner in Berlin, accustomed to always feeling like somewhat of an outsider to the cultural conversation, deprived of the experience and common history that an average German spectator has when they see any performance in their country, every new piece in the Macras factory tends to promise, almost in anticipation, a certain possibility for redemption. I can't help but get caught up, like being in a space where my native tongue is spoken. Inhabiting a house I know my way around and therefore don't have to keep asking where the silverware is or how to turn on the oven. Treading on solid ground, as the cliché goes.

It is not that her productions are especially "Argentine" in nature. This would be impossible: they are performed by a dozen dancers and actors from around the world, in collaboration with artists from different parts of the globe, at theatres that don't look anything like ours, inspired by topics that are removed from or unheard of in Buenos Aires, constructed from an assortment of elements taken from an endless stream of films, songs, and manifestations of popular culture – many of them collected from the Internet – that supraplace to which we all belong as "full experience" inhabitants of the 21st century. But, exceptions aside, in Constanza's latest productions, there is always some wink toward her country of origin that I know I am going to recognize, some song I know will remind me of my adolescence, some reference that only those of us who were raised in the same corner of the world as she was can understand in a particular manner. This is what enables me to laugh with a sense of complicity that unintentionally leaves out the rest of the audience. I can't help but feel these references were planted there especially for me: even if everyone else laughs at the same moment I do, I know they won't be doing it for exactly the same reasons. And is there anything that can invoke a greater sense of bliss than complicit laughter with another?

All revenge aside, my suspicion that *Der Palast* might include certain references that I was going to recognize straight away started to take hold in the first act, but was solidified in the second. The fictional reality show I was watching on stage had to be inspired, albeit remotely, by Bailando por un sueño [Dancing for a dream], the program that ruled prime time television in Argentina for many years. Not only was it constantly discussed on the streets, but there was also an abundance of satellite programs that undertook, from Monday to Friday, to replay and analyse what had happened on "Bailando" the night before: who had fought with whom, who seemed to be in love with whom, who had danced better (although the latter, it must be said, was the most inconsequential detail). I won't deny that all reality shows are somewhat alike, but there was a component with which I could plainly identify that Constanza was specifically referencing that show. For starters, there was something in the construction of the performers' enunciation which is difficult to put into words or transmit with concrete examples. It was more like a general flair: that pretence of integrity, that assurance of doing something important in the midst of the uproar, that kitsch constructed for the cameras, that generalized banality.

On Bailando por un sueño, the participants competed not only amongst themselves for a prize or a sense of honour, but to fulfil the dream of a charitable institution – hence the program's name. Using the judges' assessment and the audience's vote, dancing couples passed on to the next round until a winner was finally chosen. And their victory could briefly change the luck of some soup kitchen, or some NGO for children with disabilities, or some other foundation destined to cover one of the many basic needs people have in Argentina. The *Der Palast* reality show also aimed to address issues which the State should be attending to. In this case, couples dance to hold onto their houses, from which they could soon be evicted, because in Berlin things have gotten tough in recent years. The bohemian city, with absurdly low rent contracts enabling artists to concentrate on their projects without having to pay too much attention to how much money they earn, started to mutate years ago to fulfil its destiny, becoming the capital for a global powerhouse, a society identifying with the sweetness of capitalism and meritocracy.

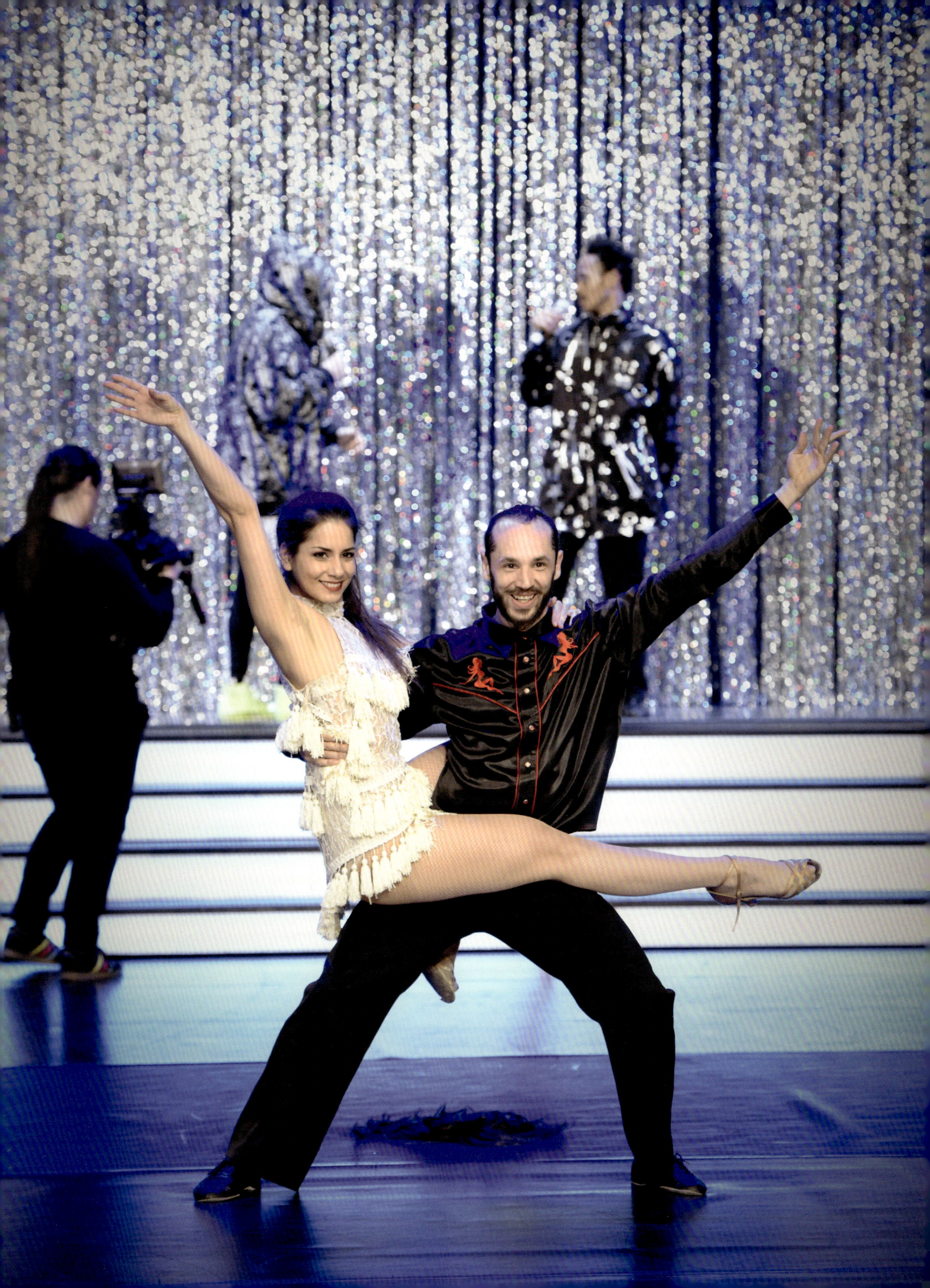

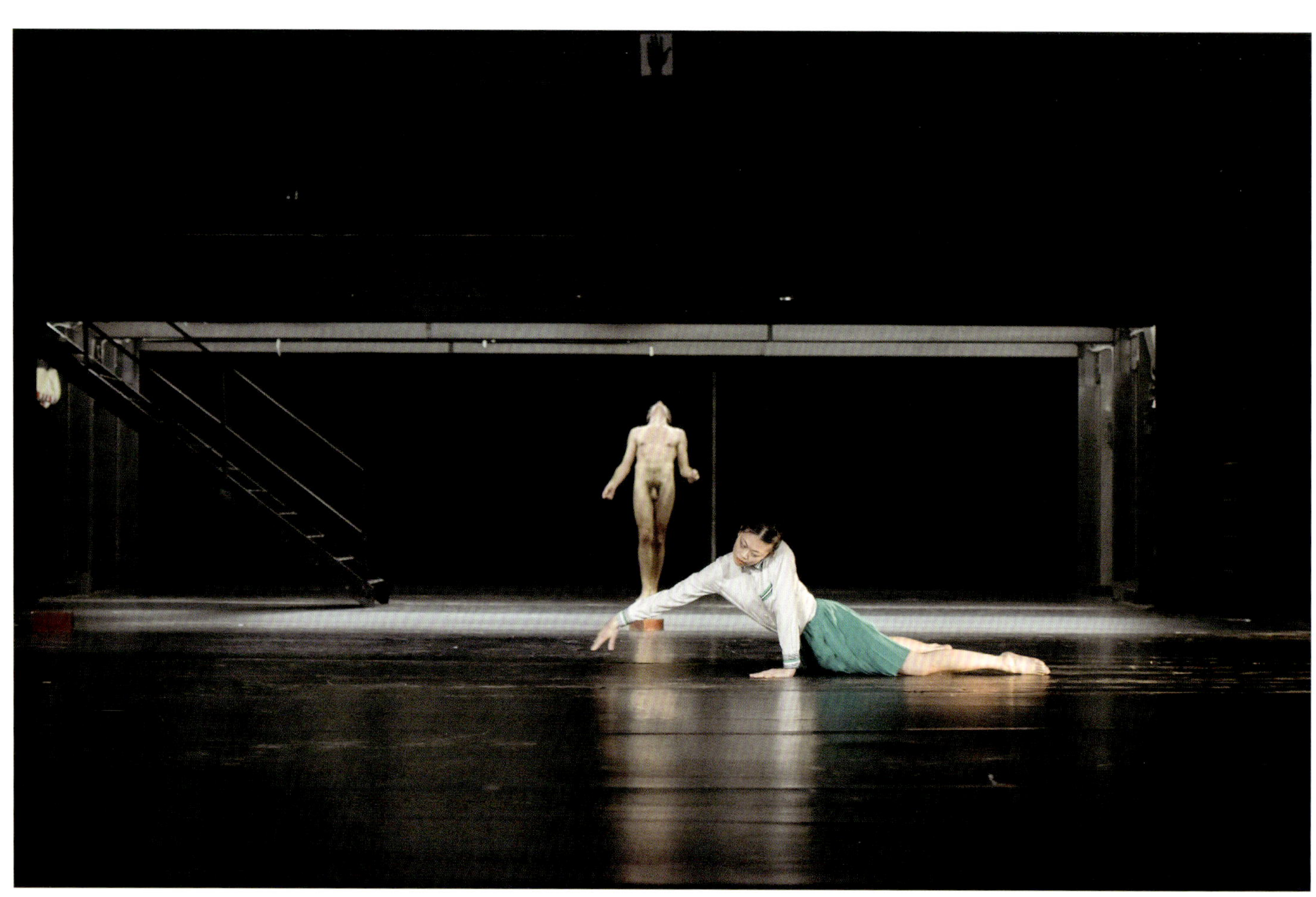

The eviction scene incarnated by Playmobil action figures in the first act of the performance symbolizes the contestants' worst nightmare. A latent and threatening nightmare, too enduring to become real at any moment.

Nevertheless, although the temptation is great, I don't want to reduce this brief essay on *Der Palast* only to the topic it takes on. Those who want to read more about gentrification in Berlin will find several testimonies in this book from real people who have been suffering from the real consequences of this problem, which started with the fall of the Berlin Wall and has accelerated in the last decade. They can also read the essay by Poligonal, or, having finished reading everything these pages have to offer, can even continue to search on the Internet, finding hundreds of journalistic articles, documentaries, and academic texts that have been circulating to give an account of this topic, which is undoubtedly concerning and scandalous. But putting our emphasis on this topic, saying that *Der Palast* is a production about gentrification in Berlin, would be minimalizing it, reducing it to the utilitarian, which I find, at the very least, unfair. Does this production have to serve for something? Is *Der Palast* responsible for making things change in Berlin? Who should the recipients of this performance be in order to generate some sort of change in the housing policy of one of the most multicultural and fascinating cities in the world?

Much more than its subject matter, I'm interested in focusing on the creative operation deployed by this show in particular, and the world of Macras in general. The operation undertaken by *Der Palast* is much more intrinsic to art, more specific to its language; it cannot be found in any academic paper, journalistic article, testimony, or urban study. By this I don't mean to say that its creative operation is better than all these other discourses; I'm just interested in underscoring its distinctive value. Although newspaper reviews often give preference to the subject matter or the utility of a production, a novel, or a film, the value of *Der Palast* vastly exceeds the good intentions that it could have. We are surrounded by films that win prizes for speaking out against racism, or novels that become best sellers for making (necessary) statements against climate change.

Constanza's work stands above the solemnity that other great works of art seem to have, or the voluntarism constructed by fictional reality show contestants in *Der Palast* – contestants who are truly convinced that they can change reality by throwing down some dance steps on television. Instead, *Der Palast* knows it is useless, knows it lacks the tools to take on the great powers that be, which, through action or omission, have brought about the current state of affairs, this present day in which not even our basic needs par excellence (a roof!) can be guaranteed for citizens in one of the richest countries in the world.

Thus, the great artistic machinery does not fail to do its job: rather than expose, it intends to draw attention to a topic firmly established in the popular consciousness that operates on and modifies the situation of hundreds of thousands of people in Berlin – and which, naturally, namely, affects minorities, immigrants, and the popular sectors. If Pina Bausch used dance to convey her performers' souls on stage, that which was inside of them, Macras uses actors, dancers, and musicians as a medium to convey that which transcends them but penetrates them, that which we could call Zeitgeist.

Before this, she spends a while reminiscing on perhaps better times, making use of one potent and fundamental visual resource in the production's aesthetic proposal: Tom Hunter's photographs, imposingly projected on the backdrop of the stage. They work to transmit the other great artistic operation of this colossal interdisciplinary project that is *Der Palast*: the hypothesis that art from the past and the urban present of the city can still coexist. At a glance, this intersection may contain a hint of nostalgia, but it is founded in a much more vital impulse: that of the will to revalue the city's public space and the different manifestations for an invitation to inhabit it. Turn it into a stage for the creation of beauty, of visual enjoyment.

And if there's anything at this point in the 21st century we can assume, it is that art can – and should – generate thought, but especially some enjoyment. Thus, the great value of *Der Palast* lies here. Even still, in a world that constantly threatens to turn against us, we continue to find a way to dance or act or take photographs or make music or enjoy those who act on stage for us. We are in wonder thanks to them. We laugh with them. We let ourselves be dazzled for a while. It is there, in that possibility – in that power – that our small revenge lies.

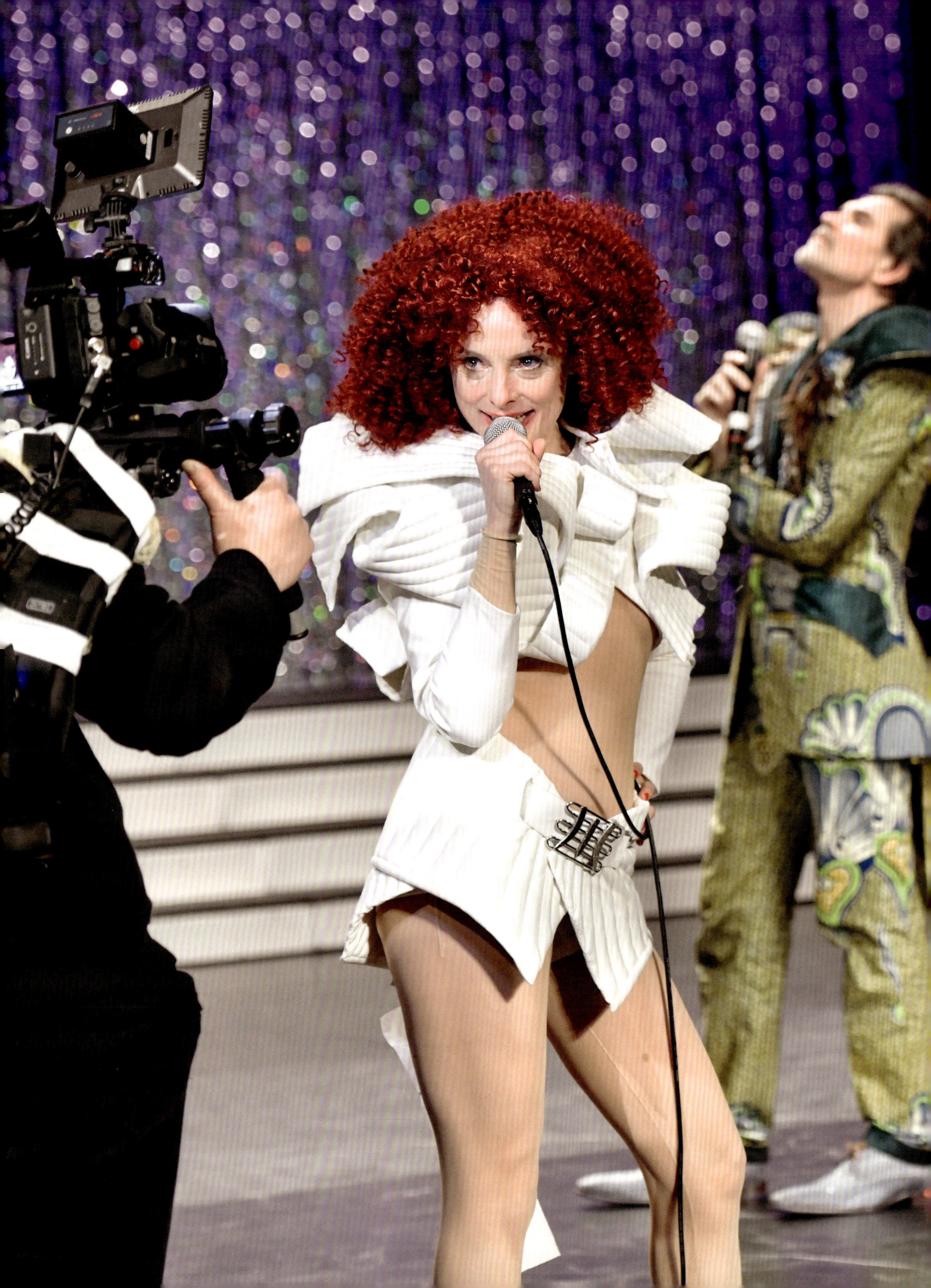

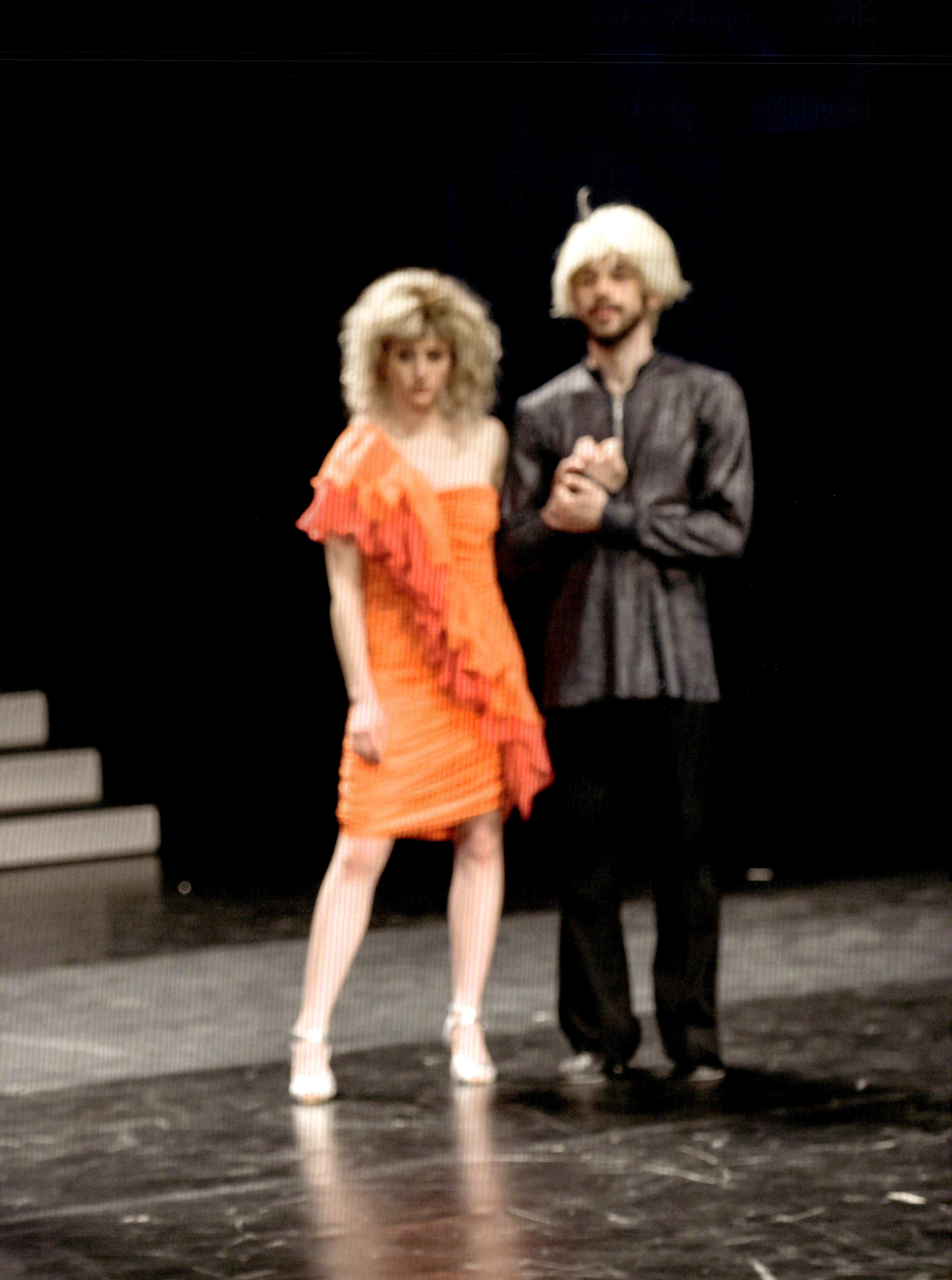

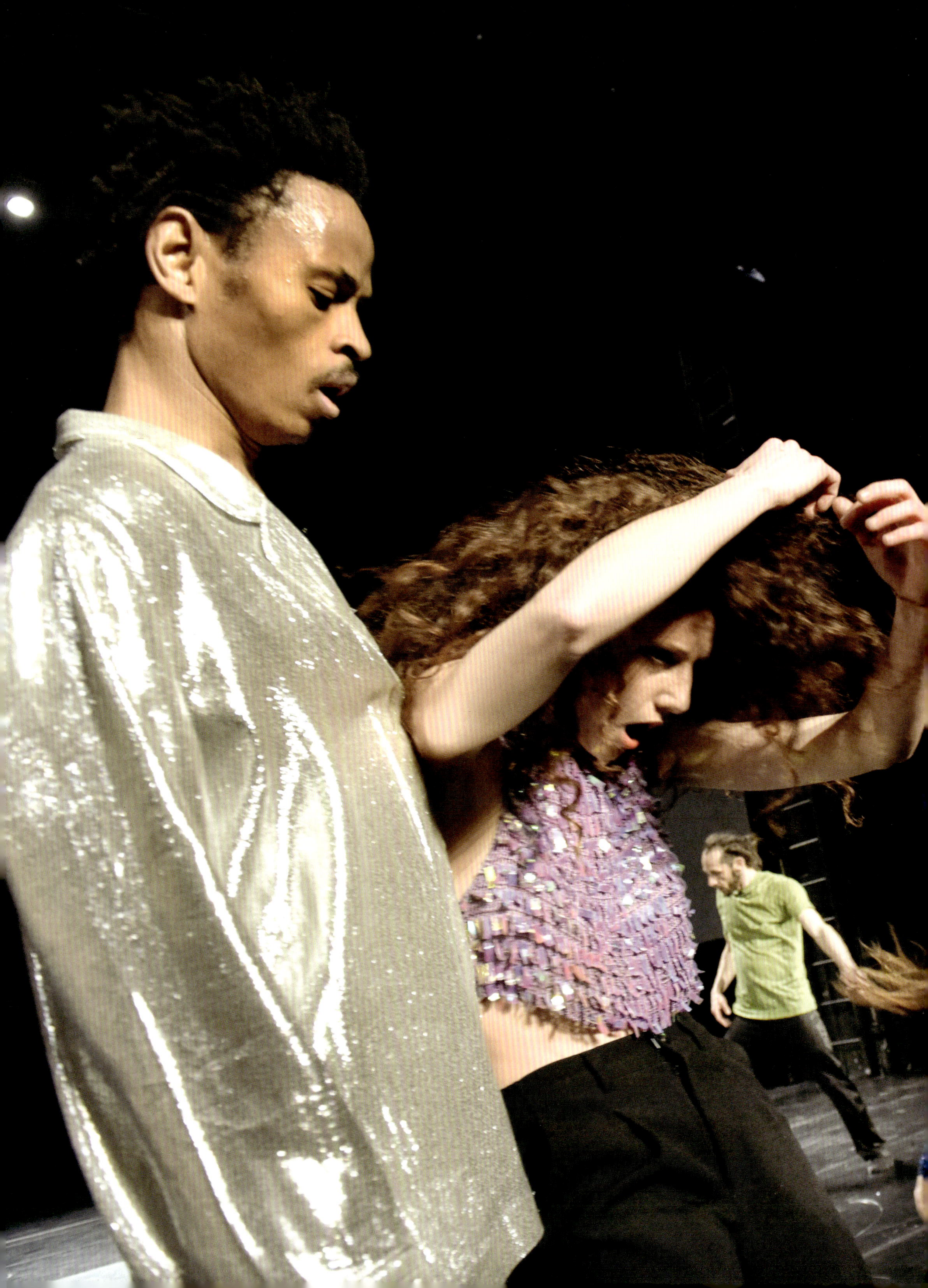

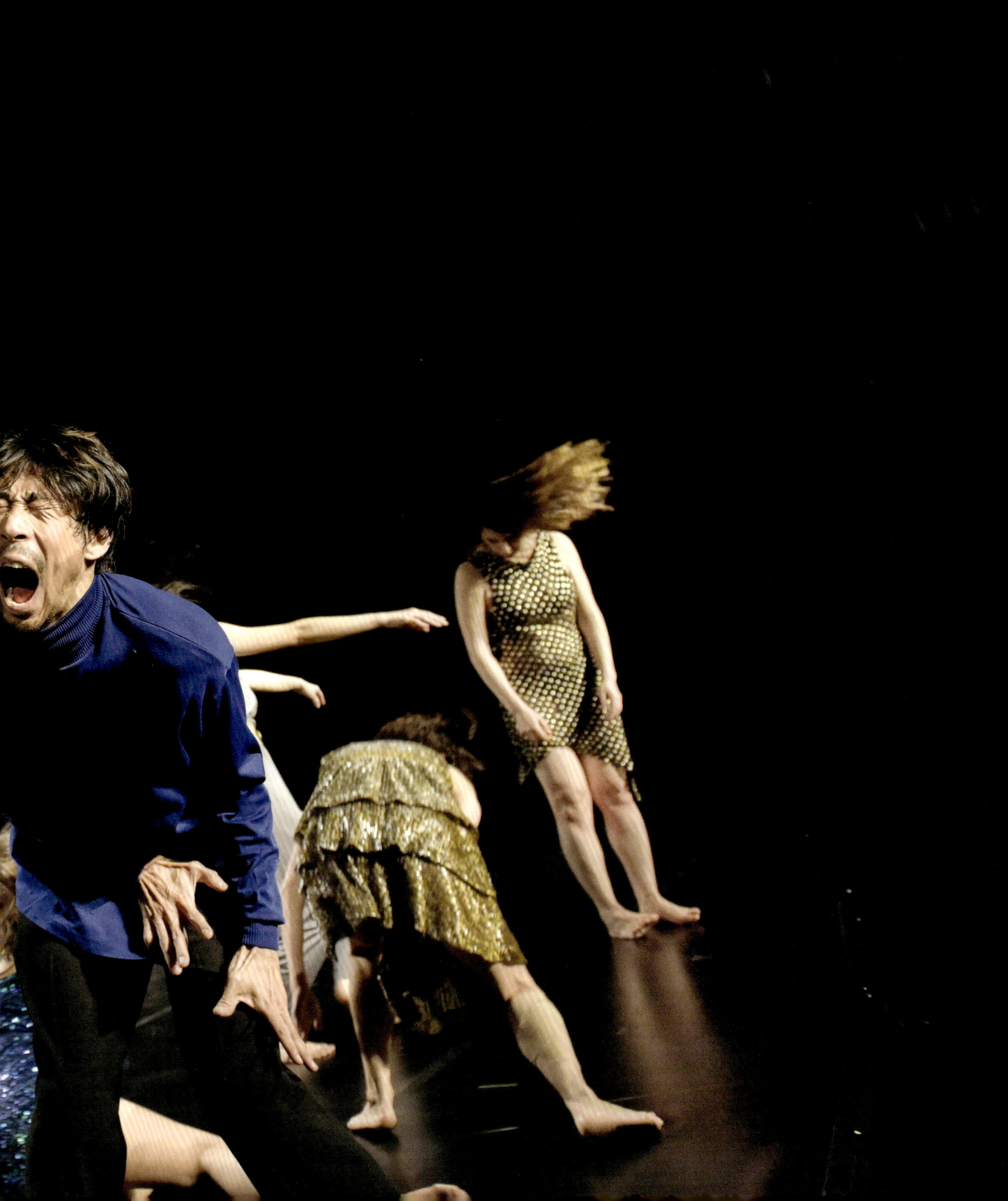

FRAU CUNTES

Songtext

Frau Cuntes
Was a lawyer
Yes a lawyer in Stuttgart
Such a prestigious job in such an rich city
The daughter would not speak to her

So Frau Cuntes left follow her son
Who lives in a WG in Berlin and smokes
lots of pot
The whole day
No it´s not a cliché, yes it is a cliché
She is retired Frau Cuntes
She is 65
And got a big pension
and what does she do with that ?

She buys a building in Helmholtz Platz
The building has rent control
Is Social Wohnung
Ay Frau Cuntes what did you do ?

She is angry because she will have to wait
for 10 years to charge a high rent…
It´s a Social Wohnung
And I tell her:
Frau Cuntes why you didn't go to retire
in Tenerife ?

Oh Frau Cuntes
You will not buy a piece of heaven this way

And tries to milk every cent she can
out of the couple moving out
a couple with a one year old son
She makes them pay for a broken tile 750 €

She remind them she use to be a lawyer
She knows the law and they have to pay

Oh Frau Cuntes you ain´t going to buy a land
in heaven this way

Frau Cuntes is bully that uses the law
As a weapon of fear
She is not an investor
She is all by herself against the social system

10 years have pass stepping on dog shit and
avoiding Laufräder Frau Cuntes
You are 75 years old and so mean
Any similarity with a real human is pure
coincidence

You could be toasting your butt in Lanzarote
But you are in Helmi writing eviction letters
In potpourri envelops
Ay Frau Cuntes you ain´t going to get a parcel
in heaven this way

Que triste Frau Cuntes
All this people…
Some of them are so old
They live in this flat for more than 30 years
Some of them drink
Where will they go
Where this people will go

Ay Frau Cuntes

Not to Gran Canaria
They don't have the choice
But you do
And they don't
Not a parcel in heaven
not a piece of paradise
For none ay any ayyy

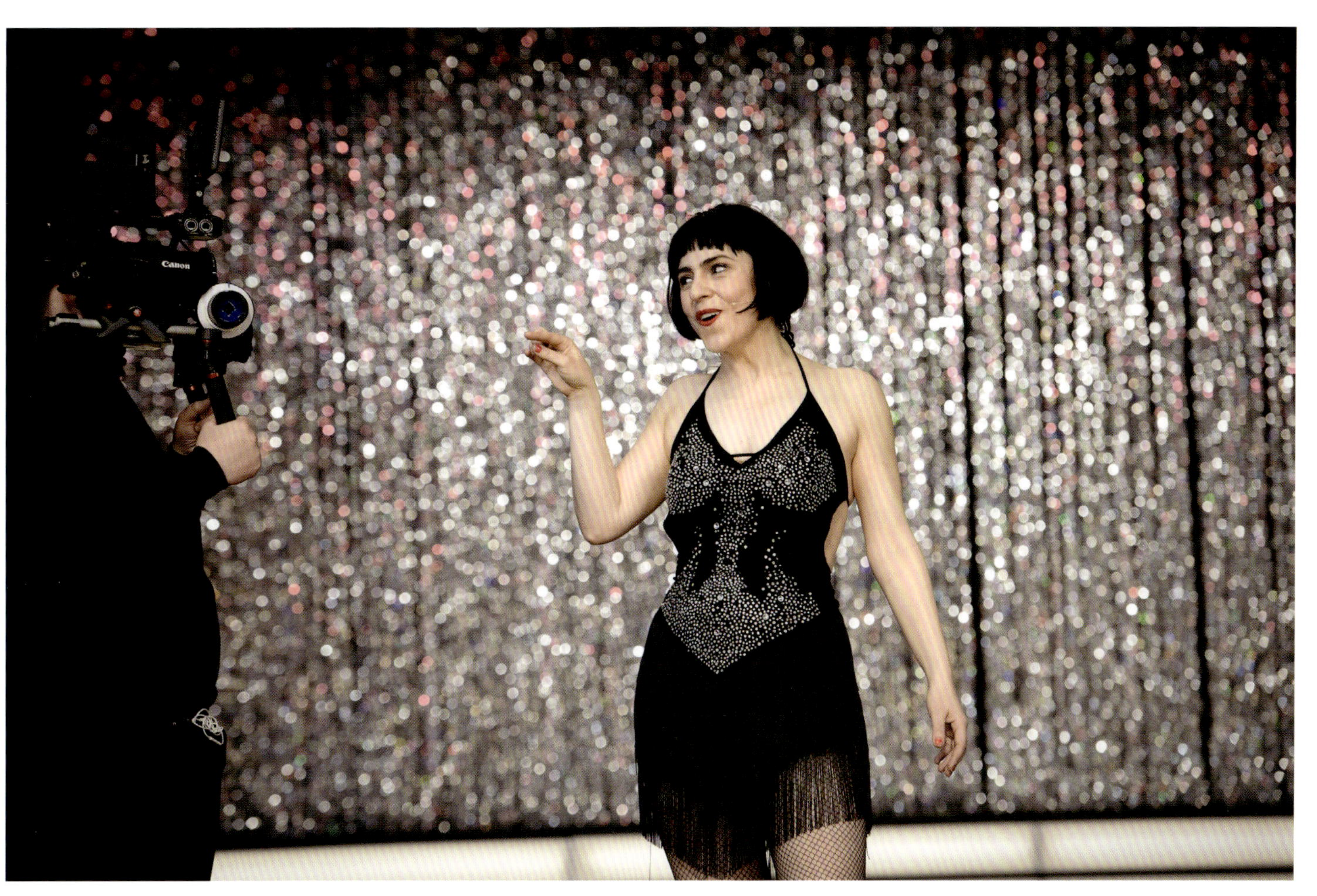

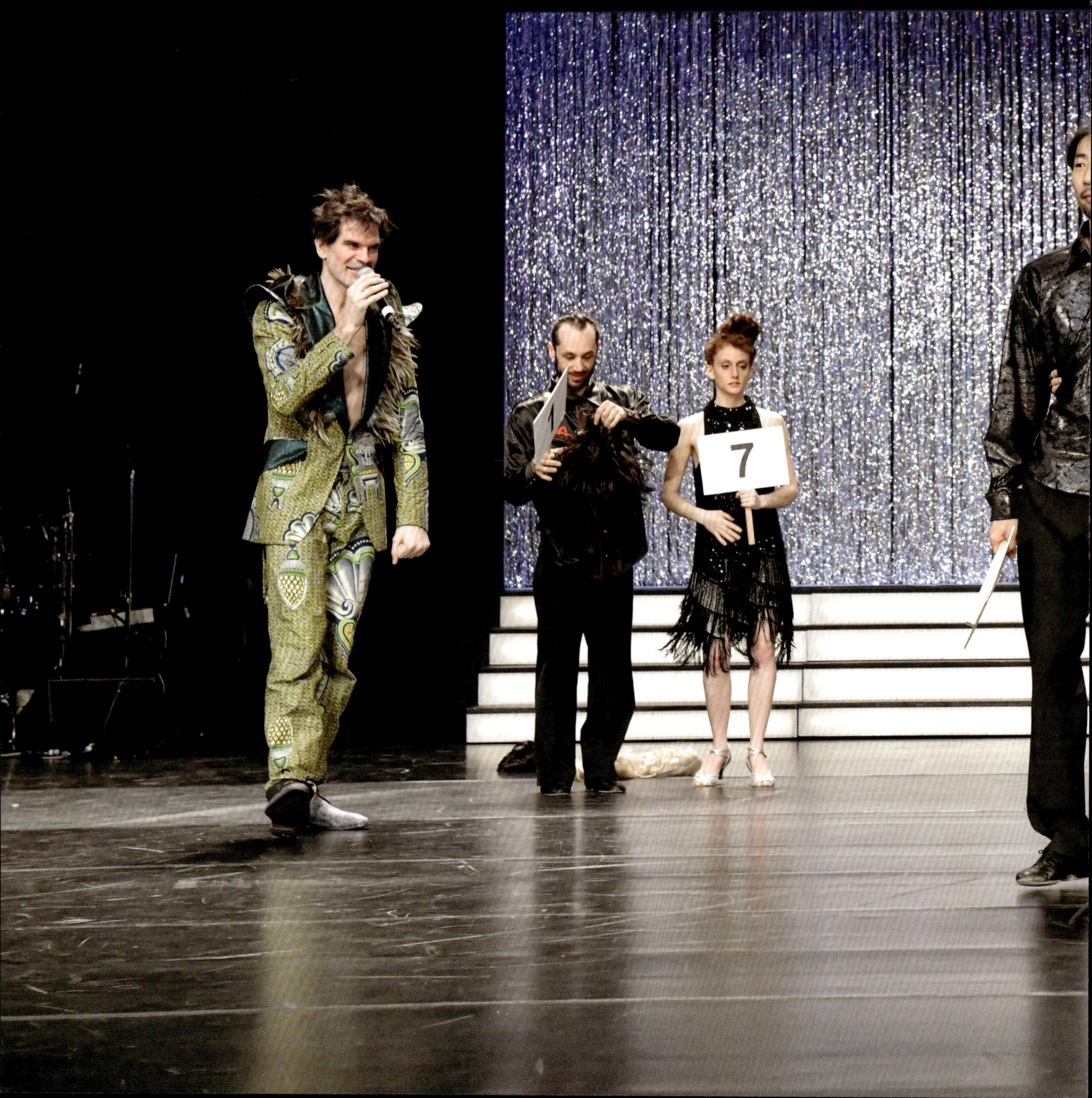

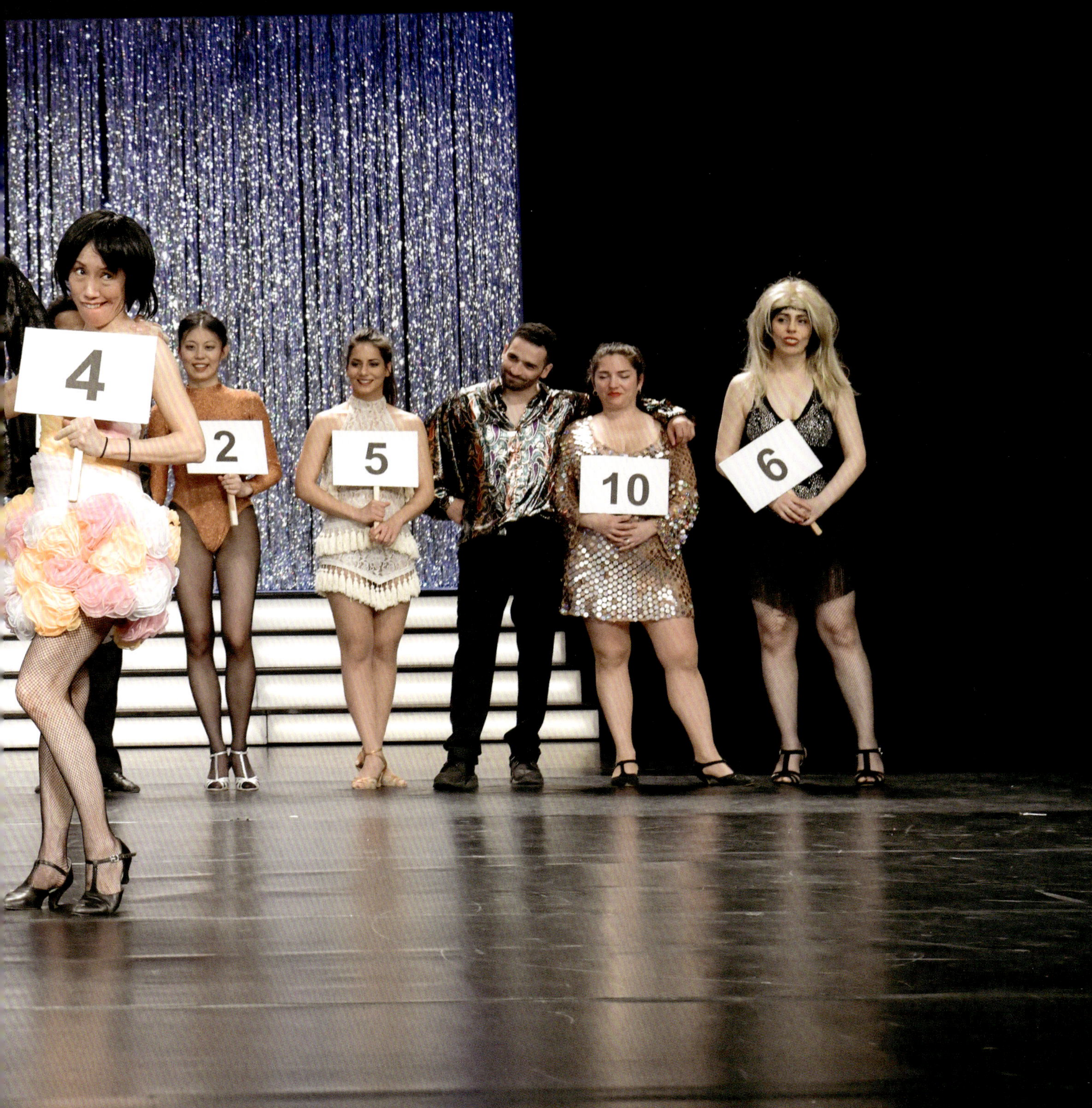

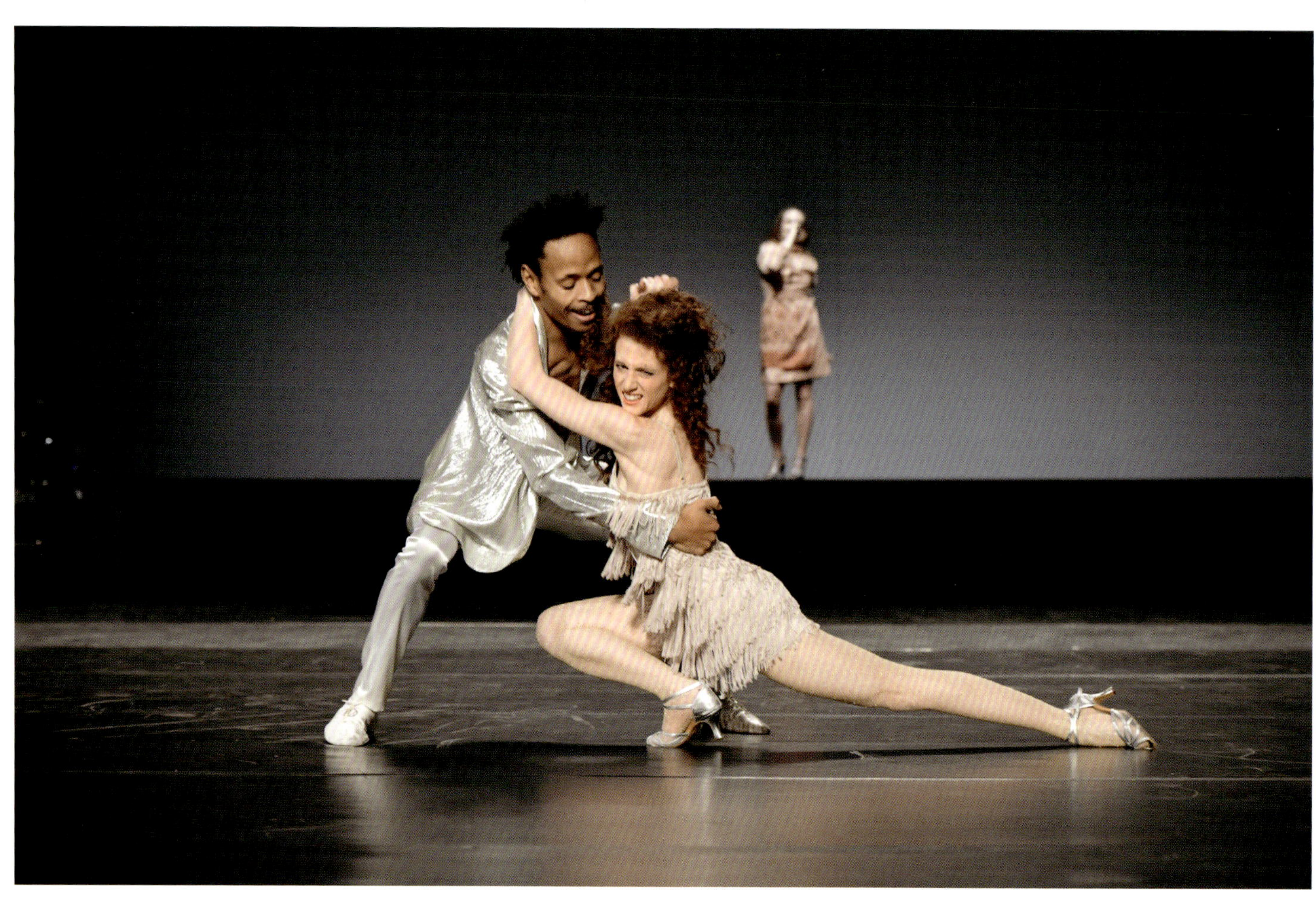

APPENDIX

REFERENCE PAINTINGS

For Tom Hunter Photographs

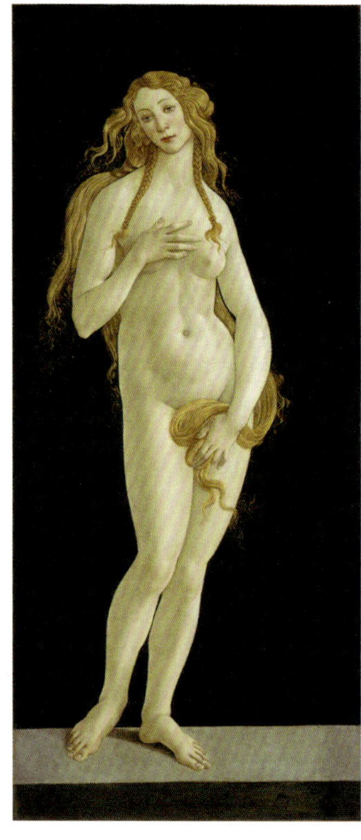

Venus
bpk / Gemäldegalerie, SMB /
Jörg P. Anders

Page 12-13

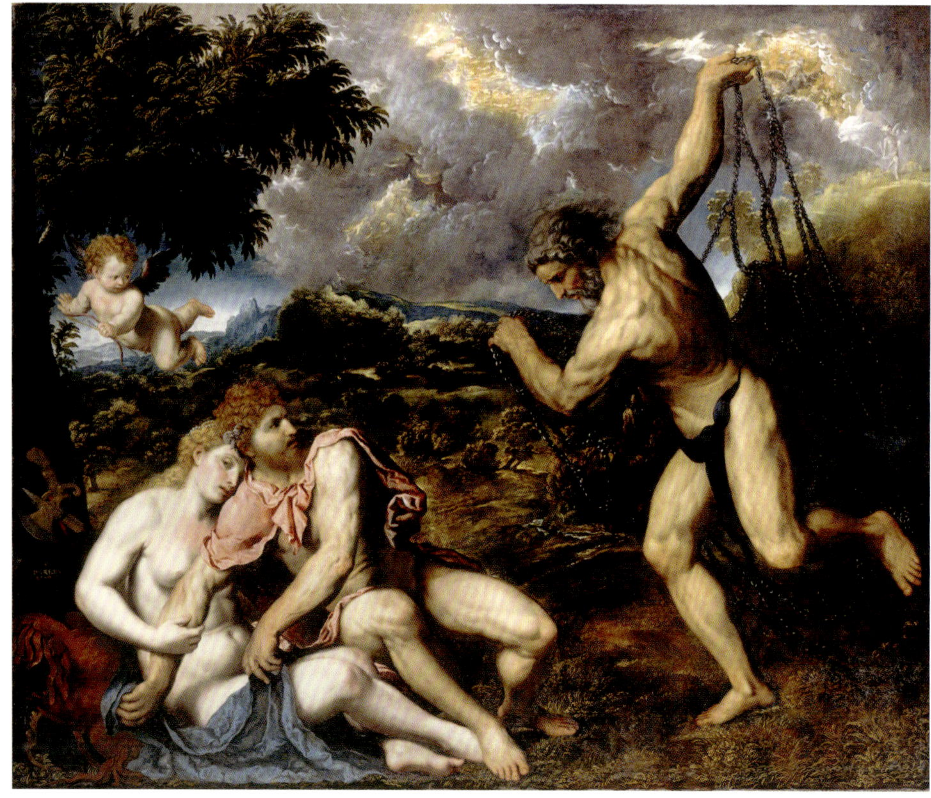

Mars und Venus,
von Vulkan überrascht
bpk / Gemäldegalerie, SMB,
Leihgabe der Bundesrepublik
Deutschland / Jörg P. Anders

Page 26-27

Leda mit dem Schwan
bpk / Gemäldegalerie, SMB
/ Jörg P. Anders

Page 16-17

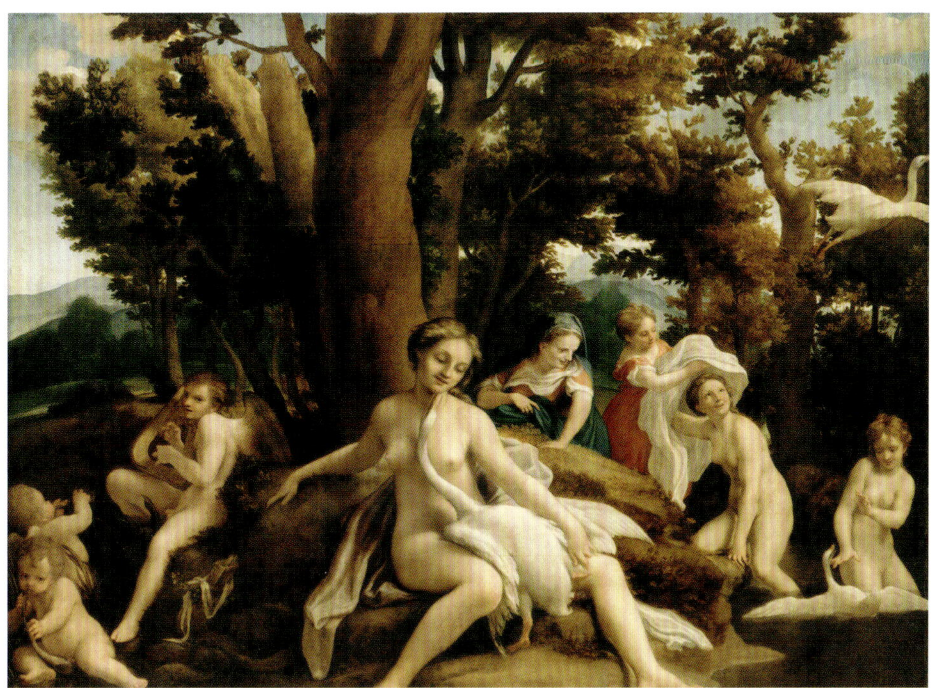

Venus mit dem Orgelspieler
bpk / Gemäldegalerie, SMB
/ Jörg P. Anders

Page 18-19

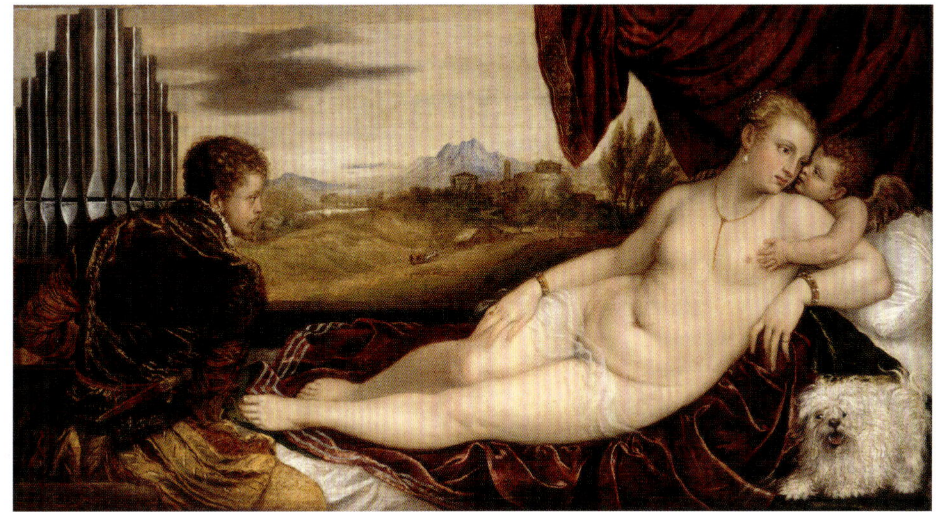

„Die Fußwaschung Christi"
bpk / Gemäldegalerie, SMB
/ Jörg P. Anders

Page 20-21

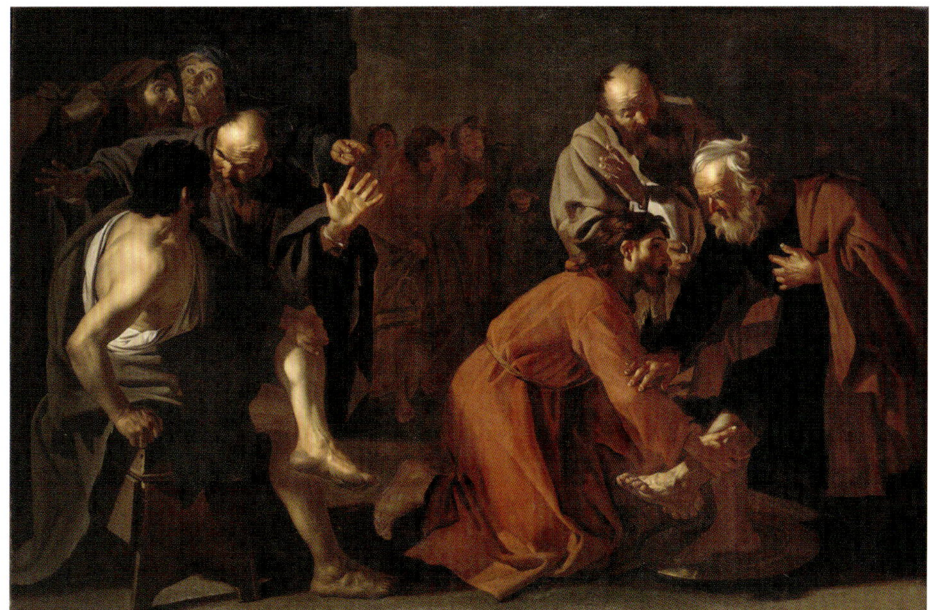

INFOS

Constanza Macras | Dorky Park Gmbh
Fahrbereitschaft
Herzbergstrasse 40-43
10365 Berlin, Germany
office@dorkypark.org
www. dorkypark.org

Distribution and International Relations:
Plan B – Creative Agency for Performing Arts
info@planbhamburg.com
www.planbhamburg.com

Book Distribution:
Alexander Verlag Berlin
Alexander Wewerkav
Fredericiastr. 8, D-14050 Berlin
info@alexander-verlag.com
www.alexander-verlag.com

Printed in Berlin, 2023
© by DorkyPark 2023

ISBN 978-3-89581-596-6

Produced by Constanza Macras | Dorky Park
Constanza Macras | Dorky Park is funded by
Senatsverwaltung für Kultur und Europa.

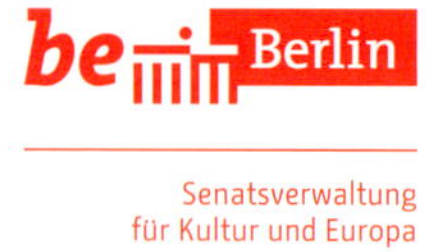

CREDITS

Show:
Concept, Direction and Choreography: Constanza Macras
Dramaturgy: Carmen Mehnert

By and with: Adaya Berkovich, Emil Bordás, Chia-Ying Chiang, Fernanda Farah,
Yuya Fujinami, Luc Guiol, Ronni Maciel, Thulani Lord Mgidi, Anne Ratte-Polle, Miki Shoji
Live music by and with: Santiago Blaum, Kristina Lösche-Löwensen, Jacob Thein
Music composition: Robert Lippok
Stage design: Alissa Kolbusch
Costumes: Roman Handt
Assistant Director: Helena Casas, Mica Heilmann
Production management: Alisa Golomzina, Xiao Yu, Jimena Soria
Production Office: Léo Pflimlin R.

Book:
Photos: Tom Hunter, Thomas Aurin
Urbanistic text collaboration: Poligonal / Christian Haid and Lukas Staudinger
in conversation with Laura Calbet Elias, Nihad El-Kayed and Sandra Oehy.
Testimonial text: Ali Yass, Daniel Magro, Marcus Smith
Interviews and Content Production: Natalia Laube
Translation „Dancing for a roof": Maureen Shaughnessy
Proofreading and Copyediting: Ena Marija Gojak
Thanks to: Simon Will

Photo Credits:
Tom Hunter: Cover, 8-9, 12-27, 30-34
Thomas Aurin: Endpaper, 38-52, Backcover

Graphic Design, Layout and Edit:
Studio SuperBlast / Manuel Osterholt

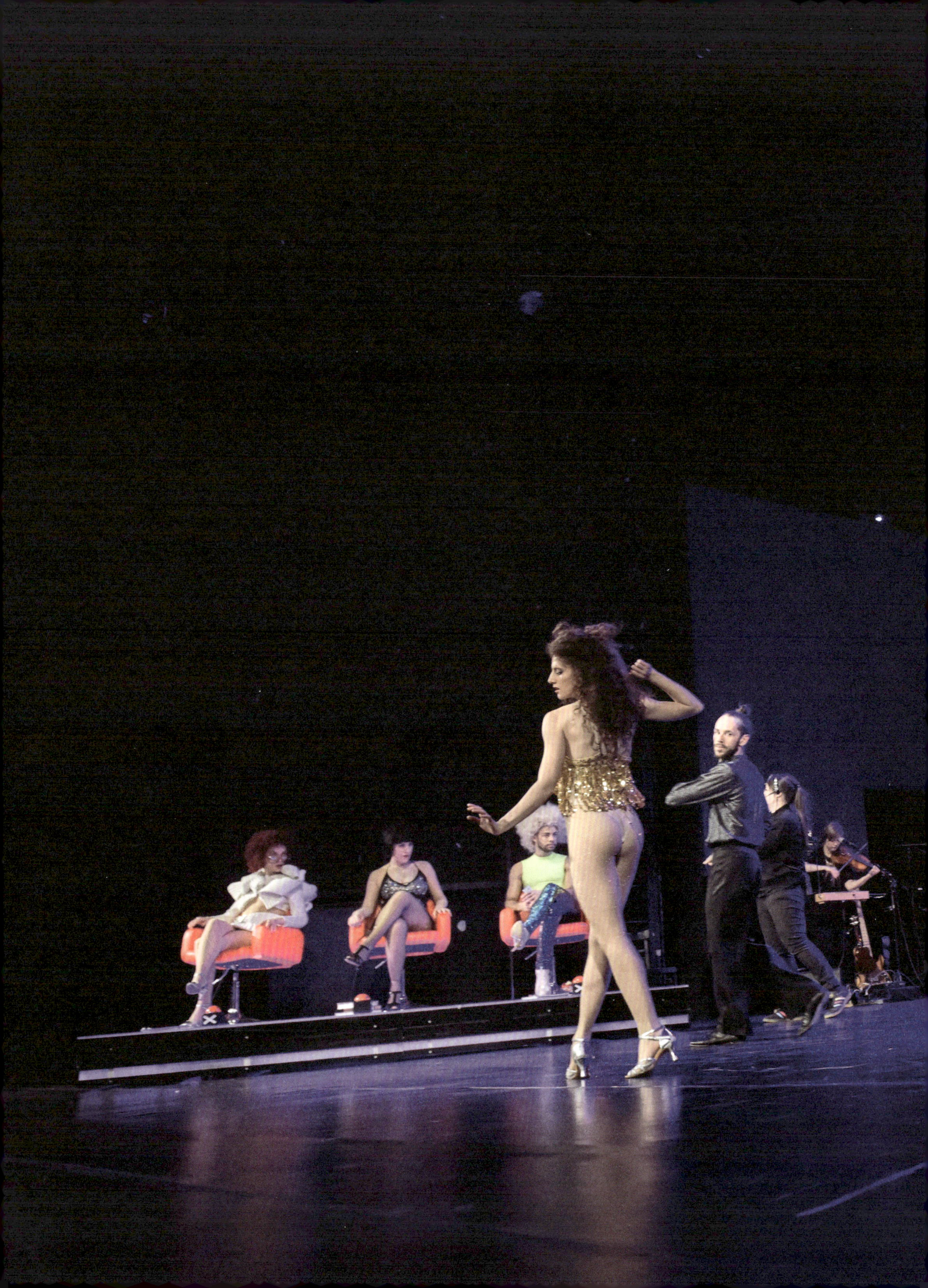